KU-279-316

MOURINHO

PATRICK BARCLAY is the chief football commentator for *The Times*. A former Sports Journalist of the Year, he has written for all the leading UK broadsheet newspapers, and travelled the globe covering the game: eight World Cups and numerous European Championships and African Nations Cups. He is the author of *Football – Bloody Hell! The Biography of Alex Ferguson* and is a lifelong supporter of Dundee FC. He lives in London.

MOURINHO

Further Anatomy of a Winner

PATRICK BARCLAY

LEABHARLANN CHONTAE
Longfoirt

L206,543/796

33406909

Copyright © Patrick Barclay 2005, 2011

The right of Patrick Barclay to be identified as
the author of this work has been asserted by him in
accordance with the Copyright, Designs and Patents Act 1988.

First published in hardback in Great Britain in 2005
by Orion Books
This edition first published in Great Britain in 2011 by
Orion Books
an imprint of the Orion Publishing Group Ltd
Orion House, 5 Upper St Martin's Lane,
London WC2H 9EA
An Hachette Livre UK Company

1 3 5 7 9 10 8 6 4 2

All rights reserved. Apart from any use permitted under
UK copyright law, this publication may only be reproduced,
stored or transmitted, in any form, or by any means, with
prior permission in writing of the publishers or, in the case
of reprographic production, in accordance with the terms
of licences issued by the Copyright Licensing Agency.

A CIP catalogue record for this book
is available from the British Library.

ISBN: 9781409134206 (HB)
9781409142607 (ETPB)

Typeset by Deltatype Ltd, Birkenhead, Merseyside
Printed and bound by CPI Group (UK) Ltd, Croydon, CR0 4YY

The Orion Publishing Group's policy is to use papers
that are natural, renewable and recyclable and made from
wood grown in sustainable forests. The logging and manufacturing
processes are expected to conform to the environmental regulations
of the country of origin.

Every effort has been made to fulfil requirements with regard
to reproducing copyright material. The author and publisher
will be glad to rectify any omissions at the earliest opportunity.

www.orionbooks.co.uk

Contents

PART FOUR
José who?

PART FIVE
Behind the mask

PART SIX
From infighting to ecstasy

Acknowledgements

It said much for José Mourinho that no one to whom I spoke in connection with the original version of this book, published in 2005 – from such giants of the football world as Sir Bobby Robson and Louis van Gaal to Andre Chin, whom Mourinho once taught at a school in Setúbal – had a bad word to say about him. Presumably, I wrote at the time, he'd had all his enemies shot.

To be serious: the man from Chelsea Football Club who told me Mourinho 'doesn't like people writing books about him without his permission' could have put his mind at rest. This was always going to be a legitimate study of a football coach and I was, and remain, deeply grateful to those important figures in the game who, understanding its purpose, gave their time and insight so generously. Robson and Van Gaal apart, they included Gérard Houllier, David Moyes and the infectiously enthusiastic, profoundly influential Andy Roxburgh.

Those who helped to bring the project up to date included Patrick Vieira and Mark Halsey.

It was a joy to obtain the thoughts of Desmond Morris and to learn from my friend Ian Ross that even a cynical old bastard can succumb to Mourinho's charm (as I was to do upon meeting him properly for the first time in Italy in 2009, when I offered him a copy of the original book in its Portuguese edition and he said he'd already bought it). Background material came from *José Mourinho: Made in Portugal* (Dewi Lewis Media, 2004). Perspective was supplied by Frank Clark and Peter Robinson, memories by Mick Martin, Ross Mathie, Tosh McKinlay and Gary Bollan. Thanks are also due to Andre Chin, Ian Aitken and to other people who spoke confidentially; to Paulo Anunciacao and Christina Lamb; to David Luxton of Luxton Harris, who guided me towards the idea; to Ian Preece, Ian Marshall and Mark Rusher for their editorial sensitivity; to James Royce for his researching and inter-viewing skills; to a truly special one, Lauren Clark, for her patience and advice; and (by no means least) to the girl with whom I share those little notebooks that mean so much.

While writing the original *Anatomy of a Winner*, I found myself warming, like so many others, to the man, while developing a distaste for some of his ways. That the dark side is still with us was emphasised by his rant after the first leg of Real Madrid's Champions League semi-final against Barcelona this spring. Yet, when people still ask if

Mourinho collaborated on the book, I suppose they are wondering what he is like at close quarters. Extremely considerate, I have found. His assistance was never sought with the book, though. There were two reasons. Mainly that the publishers wanted my hands to be free to type as they chose. But also I wanted to keep all the money.

Patrick Barclay
July 2011

PART ONE

Following Ferguson

Mayhem in Madrid

Of all the candidates named as possible successors to Sir Alex Ferguson as manager of Manchester United, only one would be utterly undaunted by the job. At least it is difficult to think of anyone other than José Mourinho to whom a sudden grinding to a halt of the Old Trafford trophy machine would involve no fear of personal failure. Mourinho has attained middle age – he will be forty-nine towards the end of January 2012 – with nothing to prove, even to himself, which is more than could have been said of Ferguson when in his own forty-ninth year, the early part of which was spent wondering if a supporter's banner telling him it was time to go back to Scotland should be heeded.

Ferguson endured much self-doubt during that winter of 1989–90, before it gave way to the spring of his first trophy in England, the FA Cup. He questioned his methods of coaching and management and entertained the possibility that he might be yet another Scot who could not live with the hotter competition south of the border. Mourinho, by contrast, breezed into England in 2004 as if he owned the place, proclaiming himself 'special' and wasting no time in proving it with two consecutive championships, a feat he had already performed in Portugal and was to repeat in Italy. He also became a European champion in Portugal and Italy. And when, having moved to Spain, he could not beat Barcelona either in La Liga or the Champions League, he gave the impression of believing that it was not the fault of either himself or his team: that sinister forces had been conspiring against his Real Madrid regime.

Those who must decide whom United should call to replace Ferguson will consider all aspects of Mourinho's character along with his record and long-term interest in the post so firmly held by his friend and senior citizen, to whom he has been known to refer as 'Boss'. The unlikelihood of his even acknowledging, let alone buckling under, the pressure of trying to maintain an unprecedented level of success achieved by a single manager in the English game would be a big plus for David Gill, the United chief executive, and any others involved in the decision to consider. The controversy Mourinho would be sure to attract, the headlines he would draw away from those who wore the red shirt, would be the minus quantity. For, although Ferguson has been an increasingly dominant and often fiery figure in the English game, requiring a firmer hand than the Football Association could ever employ, even his professional paranoia has tended to fall short of the quote delivered by Mourinho after Real Madrid had been beaten 2–0 at home by Barcelona in the acrid first leg of the 2011 Champions League semi-final. During this match Pepe, the Real player whose principal purpose of the night had been to break the lines of midfield communication between Xavi and Lionel Messi, and then Mourinho himself had been expelled by the German referee, Wolfgang Stark and Mourinho said:

'I didn't say anything to the referee. I simply laughed and showed my thumbs up. That was it. If I say to him and UEFA what I think, my career ends today. I can't say what I feel. I only leave one question. Why? Why? Why Ovrebo, Busacca, De Bleeckere, Frisk, Stark? Why to all these people?'

They were, of course, all referees whose decisions were deemed by Mourinho to have been helpful to Barcelona in prominent Champions League matches. To take various cases: Anders Frisk showed Didier Drogba a second yellow card at Camp Nou in 2005 (and was falsely accused of inappropriate behaviour by Mourinho, whom UEFA branded an 'enemy of football' and suspended from Chelsea's next two matches); Tom Henning Ovrebo denied Chelsea, now managed by Guus Hiddink, a possible three penalties in 2009 (and incorrectly sent off Barcelona's Eric Abidal); Massimo Busacca showed Arsenal's Robin van Persie a second yellow in 2011 for shooting after the whistle had blown; and, in the match that had just finished at the Bernabéu, Pepe had seen a straight red for a high challenge on Dani Alves. When Mourinho added that 'every semi-final always brings the same', he inevitably drew Frank de Bleeckere into the argument, for a year earlier the Belgian official had sent off Thiago Motta, of Mourinho's Inter, at Camp Nou (for a pushing offence that, while not as serious as Sergio Busquets had tried to make it look, followed another for which Motta had already been cautioned).

That Mourinho's theory was riddled with flaws was hardly the point, however. It was that he accused Barcelona of benefiting from a system in which UEFA and referees colluded to help them, in other words that the game was bent in favour of just one club. And he could hardly have been more emphatic. 'I won two Champions Leagues [with Porto in 2004 and Inter in 2010] with hard work, with sweat, with pride,' he said. 'I would have been embarrassed ... ashamed to win the title [as he implied Barcelona had done in 2009] because it was won with the scandal of Stamford Bridge. This will be won with the scandal of the Bernabéu. Where does all this power come from? If Barcelona are honest, they know this is happening. Sometimes I feel disgusted living in this world and earning my living in this world. It is clear that against Barcelona you have no chance. I don't understand why. I don't know if it's the publicity of Unicef [whose name was on the Catalan club's shirt], I don't know if it's the friendship of Villar [Angel Maria Villar, the Spanish football federation president] at UEFA, where he is vice-president. I don't know if it's because they are very nice, but they have this power and the rest of us have no chance.'

When this was promptly put to Pep Guardiola, the Barcelona manager had only to respond: 'I don't have an opinion on it.' He knew he had won. Or that Mourinho had lost a fight of his own making.

He had begun it in the build-up to the match, the fourth in a series of five Clasicos between Spain's great rivals, bringing up a remark by Guardiola after the previous one in which a sharp-eyed linesman had denied Barcelona a goal by a margin of 'centimetres' and making fun of it. He said: 'Up to now we have two types of coaches. A very small group who don't talk about referees and a very large group, in which I am included, who criticise referees when they make big mistakes. Now, with Pep's statement, we come to a new era with a third group, a one-person group, who criticise good decisions ... I have never seen this before.' He then began to spell out how Barcelona were favoured by decisions and made his first reference to 'the scandal of Stamford Bridge'. And on this occasion Guardiola had been unable to contain himself.

He and Mourinho went back a long way: to 1996, when Guardiola was a star player with Barcelona, his prominence in the firmament assured by a leading role in the acquisition of the club's first European title at Wembley in 1992, and Mourinho a relatively junior assistant to Sir Bobby Robson, who later said Mourinho had cultivated the popular Pep because he was clearly an influential figure around the club. They had gone on to become arguably the most successful coaches in the European game and therefore intense adversaries, even before Mourinho arrived at Real in the summer of 2010 and the Clasico quintet began a few months later with Real's five-goal slaughter at Camp Nou. Guardiola clearly felt he and his club deserved more respect than Mourinho was according on the eve of the semi-final and lost composure to the extent that he swore on television, saying: 'Normally he speaks in general terms about a club, a team. This time he said "Pep". So I say "Hey, José", in this room [the press conference], Mourinho is the chief, the fucking boss. I don't have to compete with him in here. I try not to play the game off the pitch. He is much better than me off the pitch. I represent an institution that believes this is not the best way to do things. It leaves a bad taste in the mouth. Tomorrow night there is a football match and I will see him at 8.45.'

At 8.45, Stark's whistle started a strange contest. Real stood off Barcelona, much as they had done in the final of the Copa del Rey, Spain's equivalent of the FA Cup, on the neutral ground of Valencia a week earlier, and the return Liga fixture at the Bernabéu four days before that. In both matches, the tactic had proved effective. In Madrid, despite the dismissal of Raul Albiol for the foul on David Villa that led to Messi scoring from the penalty spot, Real forced a draw through another penalty, converted by Cristiano Ronaldo. But Mourinho, correctly believing that Real could not overtake Barcelona in the Liga, had been just practising for the cup final, in which the clogging of Barcelona's channels of attack by Pepe and company again worked but, in addition, chances were made to score. In extra-time Ronaldo got the only goal with a thrilling header. Real, after nine months of Mourinho, had their first trophy in three years.

Misgivings among the Real support about Mourinho's pragmatism were receding fast and many in the crowd who gathered for the Champions League semi-final were ready to accept 0–0 if it were part of the Special One's plan. Caution, after all, was permissible if applied successfully to matches against Barcelona. On the Saturday night before this one, Real had returned to Valencia, the scene of their cup-final triumph, for a Liga match and won 6–3. The goals came from Gonzalo Higuaín (three), Kaká (two) and Karim Benzema. All three scorers were now on the bench. Pepe was back in the midfield, alongside Lassana Diarra. Angel di Maria was sent to join Ronaldo up front. Except that the team did not seem to have a front. It was set up wholly to defend, at least in the first half, which soon turned sour. Mourinho's team had been described by Guardiola as the most aggressive Real Madrid he had ever seen and, while they did not let him down, Barcelona were only too obviously ready for the tough tackling that ensued, repeatedly tumbling and appealing to Stark for justice. Eventually, after an hour, Pepe went in high on Dani Alves and yet again Real were down to ten men. Ibrahim Affelay, on for Pedro, made a goal for Messi, who flicked in the substitute's short cross before the little Argentine slalomed through the Real defence to claim a goal of such virtuosity that it was rightly compared to Diego Maradona's classic second against England in the World Cup of 1986.

Mourinho's tactical plans had been comprehensively shredded this time and, if it had been the second leg, Guardiola might have been tempted to use them as ticker-tape in the celebrations. Why had Real played so defensively on their own ground? It may be that Mourinho, fortified by his success in the cup final, had been trying to lure Barcelona's defenders forward – Gerard Piqué seldom needs an invitation and he did move into midfield several times – in the hope of getting the quick men Ronaldo and Di Maria into vacated space. But there was no service coming through and Ronaldo, who had been angrily gesturing to that effect from the early stages, pointedly remarked afterwards: 'I didn't like it, but I have to adapt to what they ask me to do.'

Meanwhile Mourinho ranted. For his dismissal to the stands, he was automatically banned from the second leg, in which Pedro scored for Barcelona and Marcelo equalised on the night. No one was sent off but Mourinho's assistant Aitor Karanka complained that Higuaín had had a goal disallowed, adding: 'Mourinho was right. He said it would be impossible for us to go through.' By then UEFA had added four matches to Mourinho's ban for a form of behaviour so inflammatory that, according to a Barcelona statement, it 'could incite violence' (a lengthy process of appeal ensued).

It was not the first time Mourinho had been accused of verging on incitement to violence. In Italy, too, he had frequently implied bias by referees, being fined in his first season for alleging that Juventus had benefited from decisions and both fined and banned for one match early in his second season for vehement protests during an Inter match at Cagliari. Four months later came a rant, after a 2–0 derby victory over Milan at San Siro, that was almost of Bernabéu proportions, and similar in character: 'Everything was done today to try to prevent Inter from winning, but my squad is strong and we will win the *scudetto*. But I will leave it at that. This is your country and your league. I am just a foreigner working here. One day, I will go and leave the problem with you. I think we all understand that it was no coincidence that the referee [Gianluca Rocchi] showed the red card to [Wesley] Sneijder.' Inter had been leading 1–0 in the first half when Lucio was shown the yellow card for diving. Sneijder approached Rocchi and applauded sarcastically until the referee understandably flourished the red. Near the end Lucio was also sent off and Mourinho observed:

'I have realised that they are not going to let us wrap this title up.'

'They' were also invoked when he talked of a decision in Juventus's favour: 'I know there is only one team [in Italy] with a penalty area 25 metres long.' Less amusing was his handcuff gesture – he crossed his wrists – and abuse of match officials after Walter Samuel and Ivan Cordoba were dismissed in a scoreless draw at Sampdoria. This, only a month after the San Siro rant, was going too far. There were hints of a strike by referees if he was not dealt with properly and the first reference to the potential gravity of the offence was made by a prominent figure in the game, Adriano Galliani, the Milan general manager, remarking: 'The attitudes of some coaches are tantamount to an incitement to violence.' Mourinho was handed his heaviest fine thus far – 40,000 euros – and a three-match ban and from there, to general relief, the storms of winter gave way to Inter's glorious spring.

Mourinho in, Valdano out

On 31 May 2010, just over a week after his tearful farewell to the Inter players with whom he had won his second Champions League, Mourinho was duly presented to the media as Real Madrid's new manager, in succession to Manuel Pellegrini. He was the eleventh in seven years but had the security of a four-year contract. Just in case anyone imagined that he might have been mellowed by the happy ending to his Italian sojourn, he said: 'I am José Mourinho and I don't change. I come with all my qualities and my defects.' And he proved as good as his word.

Not that the ousting of Jorge Valdano was necessarily evidence of a defect: the conflict between them was inevitable, if only on philosophical grounds. Valdano, a stylist under whom Real had won the Spanish title in 1995, was at the club when Mourinho arrived, working directly with the president, Florentino Pérez, as director-general and his distaste for the pragmatist Pérez had appointed surfaced after the 5–0 defeat at Barcelona in late November. Valdano noted that Mourinho had hardly left the bench during Real's humiliation by the dancing feet of a great side and remarked upon his 'inability to bring a major correction to the game'. Six months later, Valdano was gone and Mourinho perceived as all-powerful, with even Pérez singing from his hymn sheet in a way Roman Abramovich never did at Chelsea.

The strains in the relationship with Valdano were felt soon after Mourinho had arrived. Valdano made no secret that he had rejected Mourinho's request for a third striker to cover for Gonzalo Higuaín, whose fitness was in doubt. Mourinho also failed to enforce the sale of Kaká, a long-term casualty. So most of the signings for the new season were modestly priced. Mesut Özil, a star for Germany in the World Cup, cost a bargain 15 million euros, his national-team colleague Sami Khedira came for 13 million and Ricardo Carvalho, Mourinho's old faithful from Porto and Chelsea, just 8 million. The big buy was Angel di Maria, the young Argentine winger: the fee Benfica received for him would start at 25 million and probably rise to 36 as bonus clauses were activated over time.

The Liga season began with a goalless draw at Mallorca but Mourinho's Real soon got into their stride, sixteen goals coming in a trio of wins over Deportivo La Coruña, Malaga and Racing Santander. Cristiano Ronaldo was scoring regularly, jockeying for supremacy in the charts with Lionel Messi in a fascinating sub-plot to the rivalry between Real and Barcelona. The Catalans were always favourites to retain their title, however, especially after their masterclass in the first Clasico, a performance which prompted Wayne Rooney's cheerful revelation that, while watching it on television in his house near Manchester, he had found himself involuntarily rising to applaud Barcelona's gorgeous passing and movement and his wife Coleen coming in to discover what the fuss was about.

Valdano would have watched it with mixed feelings. He loved the football of the gods. In fact he played with one, being perhaps the best known of Diego Maradona's team-mates when Argentina won the World Cup in 1986, the scorer of an equaliser from the great man's pass before Maradona also played in Jorge Burruchaga for the goal that beat West Germany 3–2 in Mexico City. Valdano was a Real Madrid player at that time. After retiring in 1988, he combined media work with coaching the club's youngsters and, after being appointed manager at Tenerife, whom he guided into the UEFA Cup, he was called back to take over at Real. He later became sporting director in Peréz's first spell as president and, when Peréz was re-elected in 2009, returned as director-general and aide to Peréz. Almost as soon as Mourinho came to the club, the tension was felt and at one stage it looked as if Mourinho might be the one to lose out. Real's image suffered when he was sent to the stands by the referee of a cup match at Murcia and there were frequent exchanges with managers of other clubs, who often accused him of lacking the class associated, rightly or wrongly, with the original aristocrats of the European game.

Manolo Preciado, of Sporting Gijon, was one who took offence, describing Mourinho as a *canalla*, which roughly translates as 'low-life', for saying that his team had eased up in a match at Barcelona and asking: 'Who the hell does he think he is, saying we give up? He's a very bad colleague, an out-of-control egomaniac. If nobody at Real Madrid is going to tell him what respect means, I will. I'd like to put him up in the stands for the evening with our Ultra Boys.' Real proceeded to win 1–0 at Gijon (though Preciado and the Ultras were to enjoy record-breaking revenge in the return fixture at the Bernabéu some months later). As for Unai Emery, the Valencia manager, he responded to a Mourinho jibe that he appeared 'fragile' by saying: 'You can be very good at your job, but you should have some human values and observe them with your rivals [he mentioned Pep Guardiola in this context, along with Sir Alex Ferguson]. Then you have this guy [Mourinho] – inaccessible, disrespectful and without a minimum sense of dignity. It's to do with wanting to be the centre of attention. Is it deliberate? I don't know. In Spain there are a lot of coaches with no power, up against the ropes, and then this one arrives, with everything at his disposal. So, please, let's have a bit of respect for those who are not in such strong positions.'

Even sections of the press generally favourable to Real Madrid emitted reservations about Mourinho's personality, the *Marca* columnist Roberto Palomar writing: 'It's curious to see how Mourinho adapts the concept of "success" to whatever suits him. When it's in his interest, he unpacks his impressive list of trophies and parades them in the faces of all and sundry ... But, when the threat of failure is upon him, suddenly "success" become something relative, transient, overvalued, ethereal and mystical. So, when he's asked what would happen if Real Madrid were to lose in all three competitions this season to Barcelona, a question which makes a lot of sense after the 5–0 defeat, he prefers to turn arrogant and says it doesn't matter.'

There was trouble on the European front when it was found that Mourinho had encouraged Xabi Alonso and Sergio Ramos to collect second yellow cards, and thus one-match suspensions, in a Champions League group match once the lead over Ajax had reached 4–0 and qualification secured; they would be ruled out of the final group match against Auxerre but free again for the knockout stages. A one-match ban on Mourinho was imposed by UEFA while Real were licking the wounds Barcelona had inflicted on their pride at Camp Nou (although the threat of his missing another match if he transgressed again was later lifted on appeal). Mourinho moaned a lot, and claimed for many months that he was the only coach who had ever been disciplined for a common ploy, but he got through the winter without further traumas and the first sounds of spring could hardly have been more encouraging for him in that they came from Peréz and signified his behind-the-scenes victory over Valdano.

The president fulsomely backed Mourinho, praising him for standing up for Real's interests and pointedly adding that there was nothing 'ungentlemanly' about that. Henceforth Valdano became a marginal figure until his departure at the end of the season. Transfer policy, it was made clear, would be overseen by Peréz and his most recently appointed aide, the retired Bernabéu legend Zinedine Zidane, but with Mourinho alone making the recommendations. Politically, it was the Mourinho spring. Even if an extraordinary personal sequence of home results – not a single league defeat in 150 matches at Porto, Chelsea, Inter and Real since Beira Mar had come to the Dragão and won 3–2 in February 2002 – was brought to an end by Manolo Preciado's Sporting Gijon in early April.

His team returned to domestic form with a 3–0 victory over Athletic in Bilbao, after which, upon hearing that Barcelona had fallen behind to lowly Almeria, there was briefly hope that the deficit would be cut to five points in advance of the return Clasico at the Bernabéu. Barcelona hit back to win 3–1. But Mourinho's main focus was on the Champions League now. Real had thrashed Tottenham Hotspur 4–0, with the aid of Peter Crouch's early dismissal, in the first leg of their quarter-final and, with a semi against Barcelona as well as the Liga collision in mind, Mourinho began resting key players such as Cristiano Ronaldo, Mesut Özil and Xabi Alonso.

Continuing tension with the press, as exemplified by the journalists' walkout before the Liga match with Barcelona at the Bernabéu when they were confronted not by Mourinho but his assistant Karanka, a retired Real player who had featured in the successful Champions League campaign of 1999–2000, was put to good use. It helped Mourinho to build his customary stockade mentality among the squad. Even their 'friends' in the press, he told them, had not shown Karanka the respect due a member of the indivisible unit of which they were members.

The great Alfredo di Stefano, Real's honorary president, delivered a gloomy verdict on the 1–1 draw at the Bernabéu – 'Barcelona were a lion, Madrid a mouse' – but the mouse was about to roar as Real took the Copa del Rey, ultimately in style, Angel di Maria crossing so superbly in the 103rd minute that he twitched with anticipatory excitement even as the ball curled towards Ronaldo, whose rocket of a far-post header left Victor Valdes helpless. Di Maria's subsequent departure after a second yellow card was of limited relevance. This meant that Mourinho's great rival Guardiola had failed to win three of the trophies available to Barcelona over his three seasons to date – and that Mourinho, first with Inter in the Champions League, had denied him two of them.

L206,543/96
334069092
LEABHARLANN CHONTAE Longfoirt

Afterwards, Mourinho said: 'I am happy that our work is paying off.' And later, asked how he had repaired his team after the 5–0 defeat, he replied: 'What I've said to my players is simply – and these are not my words but the words of Albert Einstein – that the only force that is more powerful than steam, electricity or atomic energy is the human will. And that guy Albert is not stupid.'

This was on the eve of the Champions League first leg, amid all the taunts that so irked Guardiola. But the human will, it turned out, also drove Barcelona.

Yet, even as the wider world ridiculed Mourinho's paranoid reaction – 'He seems to get worse every year,' said the Sky Italia commentator Massimo Marianella – and UEFA prepared to exert discipline, it became clear that he had not entirely lost the battle for Madrid's hearts and minds. In London, *The Times* sought a pro-Mourinho view from the Spanish capital and Jesus Alcaide, a columnist for *El Mundo*, was only too enthusiastic. He began with sarcasm – 'it is very possible that in the next few days José Mourinho will be accused of war crimes and have to appear before the International Court at The Hague' – and concluded: 'Madrid is with Mourinho and will defend him to the death in front of UEFA and in front of anyone. The Portuguese's words have struck a chord because he works and he lives for the club. The feelings are mutual. It will be long-lasting.' Alcaide also warned Manchester United to prepare to play ten versus eleven in the final at Wembley, because they would surely have someone sent off against Barcelona. In fact the Wembley event turned out to be an extremely sporting encounter, after which Sir Alex Ferguson generously praised Barcelona and said there was no shame in his players losing 3–1 to such an exceptionally fine team. The contrast was telling.

At least Ferguson's season ended at the highest level. Mourinho's petered out after the 1–1 draw in second leg of the semi-final with the boss absent and Karanka echoing his master's voice in a valedictory complaint about a refereeing decision. *The Times*, as if slightly ashamed of having given space to the devil's advocate Alcaide, left us with a brilliant piece by its chief sports writer, Simon Barnes, who declared that Mourinho's rant had made it plain that he was not, after all, a lovable eccentric or a maverick genius but 'just the loony on the Tube: change carriage at Aldgate East because he's going all the way to Barking'. Mourinho had the great talent possessed by quite a few egomaniacs, wrote the perceptive Barnes: that of enforcing on others the duty to gratify his whims. But now was the time to stop listening to him and slip away 'because the next time you meet he'll tell you he's Napoleon'.

That might have been how many in England had come to see it, and in Italy and the rest of Europe. In Manchester, not least. His next port of call, after Madrid, was widely expected to be Manchester, where City were now funded by one of the richest men in the world,

Sheikh Mansour bin Zayed Sultan Al Nahyan, but where Mourinho's own inclination had long been to take the place of his friend Sir Alex Ferguson at United. Would United have wanted a man who screamed red murder in adversity – or who set up a team so defensively, so cynically, at home in a Champions League semi-final? The feeling among supporters about Mourinho had always been ambivalent; this tended to confirm the instincts of the sceptical faction and David Gill, as much as anyone connected with the club, would have been aware of it. Not that the item was at the top of United's agenda; in the wake of the Champions League final defeat by Barcelona, the word from the club was that Ferguson, seven months short of his seventieth birthday but in apparently excellent health, had indicated a wish to stay for another three years. So Mourinho's stock had fallen on the international market. But Madrid was still with him because, although Guardiola had the Spanish and European titles for the moment, Mourinho retained the anatomy of a winner.

Quietly, as the rest of the world hailed Barcelona's magnificent 3–1 victory over United at Wembley – at times the performance had reached the heights of the season's first Clasico – Mourinho continued assembling his squad for the new campaign. The Turkish/German influence already evident through Ozil and Khedira, who represented Germany despite their families' origins, was enhanced by the securing of two members of Turkey's midfield: Nuri Sahin, a 22-year-old from Borussia Dortmund who cost 10 million euros, and the 28-year-old Hamit Altintop on a free transfer from Bayern Munich. José Maria Callejón, a 24-year-old technician, came from Espanyol for 5.5 million. Then the capture of a coveted French teenager, the tall defender Raphael Varane (10 million from Lens) was followed by the most expensive arrival of the summer to date, the left-sided Portuguese full-back or midfielder Fabio Coentrao (30 million from Benfica). The buys from a year earlier came while Mourinho was getting his feet under the table.

These now, were definitely his.

The departure of Valdano had left no doubt that Mourinho would be both architect and builder of the 2011–12 season at Real. His last in Madrid? We would have to wait and see but, according to the English referee who had become perhaps his most surprising friend – he got close to Mark Halsey after the Englishman had treatment for cancer – it was only a matter of time before Mourinho returned to the Premier League. 'Oh, he'll come back,' said Halsey as the controversy raged over the Bernabéu allegations. 'He's got his life all mapped out. And let's just hope it's sooner rather than later, because the Premier League is missing him. Chelsea have definitely gone backwards without him.' Halsey's admiration for Mourinho was understandable: when Mourinho was at both Inter and Real, he invited the Halsey family to be his guests at matches and the referee conceded: 'If he came back here while I was still on the senior list, I wouldn't be allowed to ref his team.' But much of what Halsey said about Mourinho's personal qualities helped to explain why players swear such fierce allegiance to him; Xabi Alonso, for instance, declaring: 'From an emotional point of view, he is very strong. He makes each player the best he can be. He knows how to connect with us.'

Halsey said: 'I've been fortunate enough to be taken round Madrid's training ground by him twice, and you can see that the players have so much respect for him. He has the players eating out of his hand. The way he manages people is fantastic. A lot of people, in every walk of life, could learn from José Mourinho about how to manage people by treating them properly and looking after them. Unfortunately many managers, not just in football but in other spheres, come nowhere near his standard. He's been an absolute inspiration to me and my family. I suppose that, for someone like myself who's grown up and gone through life without a father [Halsey's father left his mother when he was a toddler and they did not meet again until Halsey was in his thirties], the sort of man you would want would be José Mourinho. Well, I would, anyway. If I could choose a father, he would be the man.'

Which takes us back to the year after they met. The year in which Mourinho brought his children to England.

PART TWO

Welcome to England

He does what it says on the tin

It was near the end of 2004, the year in which English football had encountered its most startling new manager since the first flush of Brian Clough.

As Christmas approached and the people on London's streets retained, for just a few more days, a blissful ignorance of the word 'tsunami', a couple living in one of the more prosperous and fashionable districts of the capital decided to take their two children ice-skating. Each year a rink was created in a little square of shops just off the King's Road and, while it might cross a certain kind of mind to observe that the happy-family atmosphere engendered must be good for business, even such a cynic would find the remark freezing on pursed lips. For pre-Christmas crowds have a refreshing lightness of heart. Nuts and oranges may have given way to technological toys as the tokens of seasonal generosity, but the traditional spirit survives and, liberated by it, people reacquaint themselves with their best instincts in smiling at strangers or apologising when they might otherwise grimace. And our couple, to whom the experience of a Christmas in London was new, were obviously enjoying a rare afternoon as a family.

Each holding a child by the hand, they moved through the shoppers to the edge of the ice, where the girl and boy – she about nine years of age, he about five – were helped to put on their skates. Even muffled against the cold, the father attracted a few glances of recognition, but famous people, footballers among them, have often said that one of the benefits of coming to London is that they are not harried in the street and can live a relatively normal life (at least as normal as most of them would wish it to be), and this respect was accorded our man. One admirer took a photograph from such a distance that the subject would not have noticed. The only person who approached José Mourinho was a Portuguese football writer resident in London who knew him slightly and who, having wished him and his family a happy Christmas, withdrew to attend to his own wife and small son.

Mourinho leant back on a wall to watch as the boy and girl skated off, she confidently and he less so. Mourinho would check on them and, usually, upon returning to his wife's side, he would kiss her. He frequently called to the children, encouraging them and, with signals, offering suggestions on how they could improve their technique. From time to time, like most of the other children, they fell and on one occasion the boy had difficulty in rising from the ice. Immediately Mourinho was with him, offering not a helping hand but a demonstration of the best method of getting up. He waited while the boy followed his advice, smiling patiently. And off the boy went again, with more assurance. Anyone who saw the incident would have formed the impression that Mourinho was a sensitive father. Which in turn provided a hint as to why he had made such an impact on football.

For at the highest level of management these days – and henceforth we shall fall into line with most of the world and refer to Mourinho's field as coaching – sensitivity rules. And, for all the peevishness that was to get him into trouble with both authority and the media, Mourinho takes care of his players.

'I like the look of Mourinho,' Clough had said shortly before he died. 'There's a bit of the young Clough about him. For a start, he's good-looking ...' Which indeed Clough had been in his early days at Derby County, before the booze began to blur his sharp features and mottle his complexion. But times have changed and you cannot boss a player around as easily as Clough might have done, or use the discipline of estrangement from his peers by sending a star to train with the youth team, as Clough once did. Most coaches have to accept that Sir Alex Ferguson, who could lash out at a stray boot and send it flying through the dressing-room air, drawing blood from one of David Beckham's expertly plucked eyebrows – and proceed, with total impunity, to sell the then England captain to Real Madrid – represented the end of the line. One by one, culminating in the European Court case won by Jean-Marc Bosman in December 1995 that allowed players to move freely at the end of their contracts without their new employers having to pay a transfer fee, the constraints have been stripped away.

To claim that Ferguson and his predecessors – the likes of Sir Matt Busby at Manchester United, Bill Shankly and Bob Paisley at Liverpool, Don Revie at Leeds United, Bill Nicholson at Tottenham Hotspur and even Clough at Derby and Nottingham Forest – were mere martinets would be as misleading as to imply that Mourinho and Arsène Wenger, outstanding exponents of the modern style of coaching in England, have been indulgent softies. It would also do an injustice to the multi-dimensional nature of the job. Aime Jacquet, who coached France to victory in the World Cup in 1998, touched on this when he said: 'Today children are more curious and bolder. That is why we have to prepare coaches not just to teach youngsters about what happens on the pitch but about psychology, physiology, drugs, doping and social education. The coach of the future will have to be at different times a teacher, a buddy, a father, a friend, etc. It will not be enough for him simply to impose authority. He will need above all the ability to listen and pass on a message. He must be credible and able to defend his values.'

You may think those words a reasonable description

of the role of today's youth coach, not applicable to those charged with guiding the aristocrats of modern football who earn their livings with Mourinho at clubs with the lavish budgets of Chelsea, Internazionale or Real Madrid. Until you remember that during his first few months at Stamford Bridge he had to deal with the distraction created by the Romanian attacker Adrian Mutu's cocaine problem. Eventually, Mourinho ran out of patience. Mutu was tested by the club, sacked, named and shamed and, after a spell in limbo, went back to Italy, where he joined Juventus. The message was clear: cross Mourinho, abuse the friendship of this buddy, and the only way was out (and an expensive direction it proved in Mutu's case, for Chelsea pursued a claim for damages and he was ordered to pay £15 million).

The modern coach must strike a balance between strength and sensitivity. Mourinho contrives to be both things to all men. That is part of the reason he is – to use his own word – special. Should he have said it? Should he have breezed into England and inspired a classic *Sun* headline – 'The Ego Has Landed' – by telling the press that Chelsea could be champions because they had terrific players and a 'special one' as coach? His own justification, outlined at the end of the season in a BBC television interview with Gary Lineker, was that he had suddenly found himself in a strange environment being showered with questions by people who seemed to be hankering for his credentials. Anyway, it was a statement of fact that he offered them rather than a grandiloquent aspiration; there are not many coaches who have won the UEFA Cup and Champions League in their first two full seasons with a club, sweeping up a couple of national championships and a domestic cup along the way, but that is what Mourinho had done with Porto in his native land.

Some eighteen months later, when he had encountered the fall from grace examined later in this book – Mourinho's moaning after a defeat by Barcelona in the Champions League at Stamford Bridge led Hugh McIlvanney in the *Sunday Times* to dub him the Specious One – he was to leave himself wide open to such mockery. But in the early summer of 2004 his image was untouchable.

In the stadium in Gelsenkirchen, Germany, where the Champions League final was won by Porto, he had spoken of his need for a fresh challenge. He had spoken with ambition and, overwhelmingly, of himself, and perhaps it was because of this that I, along with other journalists in England, got off on the wrong foot. It was not that his achievements could be belittled, more that the history of football was strewn with instances of success through chemistry – Arrigo Sacchi developed the formula for a great Milan, but nothing as explosive afterwards – and it looked as if this Mourinho chap was sorely tempting fate. The press were not alone in wondering if his pride came before a fall. The coaches waiting to pit their wits against him in the Premier League felt it too. One of the brightest, David Moyes, who was also to enjoy an outstanding season as Everton qualified for the Champions League by finishing fourth, recalled relishing the prospect of Mourinho's comeuppance. 'The initial feeling,' Moyes told me some months later, with a smile and a sigh, 'was that you just couldn't display that kind of arrogance in this country and get away with it. I think there were a few queueing up, you know, waiting to have a crack at him.'

We the professional bystanders did not hesitate to have fun with him. Such was his self-absorption (I wrote) that he would fit perfectly into contemporary London. I imagined him cutting a swathe through the traffic in a massive black 4x4 with smoked windows which, having stopped and carefully straddled two parking bays in order to reduce the risk of scratches from other vehicles, would disgorge the smooth operator, suit miraculously uncreased and mobile-phone cord dangling from one ear as details of the next day's training were laid down to a distant underling.

Well, I didn't know he was kind and attentive to his children, did I? I didn't know he would nuzzle his wife by the ice-rink wall when no one was looking. I didn't know the country would take such a liking to Mourinho that, by the Christmas of 2004, it could be asserted that he was the most admired football personality of the day among neutrals and followers of his own club alike: a position that had fallen vacant because Newcastle United had seen fit to part company with Sir Bobby Robson, Mourinho's old boss and guide.

Far from tempting fate with his high self-esteem, Mourinho had taken fate in his hands and, as in Portugal, shaped it. I think that is the main reason we warmed to him: to borrow the brilliant simplicity of television commercials for Ronseal, a range of products including varnish and woodstain, he did what it said on the tin. In England we had become used to a culture of in-efficiency or, to use the expression favoured by football folk, sloppiness. When a train turned up on time, we were pathetically grateful. When we arrived home with a bag of oranges, tore the netting apart and found every single one to be rot-free, we almost burst into tears of joyous relief. Things went wrong, sometimes horribly wrong. Hideously wrong. At the time of Mourinho's arrival, anyone who emerged from a public hospital no worse than when he or she went in was assumed to have supernatural powers. Nor was this the only cause for public dismay. A war was conducted on the basis of 'intelligence' used without due care and attention. Small wonder that, in the build-up to the general election of May 2005, the key issue was to be identified as not health or education or security so much as the ability of any of the parties to deliver any promise at all. So little could be taken on trust. For many people, life in England had become a matter of hoping for the best.

Even in football, an activity rare in that it still inspired unrealistically high expectations, the customers' charter could not be relied upon to guarantee same-day delivery: why, the poor dears who supported Manchester United and Arsenal, the clubs who had established a clear superiority over all others since the Premier League was formed in 1992 (or the top division of the old Football League hived off and rebranded, as some of us might insist), had been obliged to share the intoxicating nectar of supremacy with each other. It was the beginning of a particularly cruel era in football. The language of the phone-in, later to be taken further downmarket by the internet chatroom, had become prevalent. Coaches of clubs from Tyneside to the south coast lost a couple of matches in succession and were decried for having lost much more than that; they had lost 'the plot'. In front of packed houses, the majority of teams 'underachieved'. Leeds United and others ran up vast debts 'chasing the dream', egged on by fans who, when the dream turned out to be a financial nightmare, immediately accused the directors of reckless extravagance.

Chelsea were among those who lived beyond their means in the early years of the twenty-first century. Until a small proportion of the riches Roman Abramovich had made – through Boris Yeltsin's shameful car-boot sale of the Russian people's oil and gas, let us never forget – was applied to an eminently unworthy cause, the saving of a football club's skin. The saving, moreover, of a club that had reached the verge of ruin under Ken Bates. To give Bates his due, that was the condition in which he had found Chelsea in the first place, and he left it much more robust than had been the case a quarter of a century earlier, when he was able to buy it for £1. But the advent of Abramovich still rendered Bates the luckiest man in football and, having taken the near £20 million the Russian gave him for his shares and tried to settle in Monte Carlo, he soon got bored and returned to England to apply his unique abilities to the erstwhile dream-chasers of Leeds.

Chelsea were, on the face of it, even luckier. They had been plucked from the jaws of bankruptcy and turned overnight into the world's most financially muscular club (a title they retained until Manchester City were bought by the fabulously rich Sheikh Mansour of Abu Dhabi). While Claudio Ranieri stayed as coach for one more year, clinging to his dignity with one hand and a negotiating position with the other, Peter Kenyon, the chief executive Abramovich had lured from Manchester United, courted the England coach, starting at what we can only presume he mistook – rather in the manner of an inexperienced mountaineer – for the peak of the profession. It was just a ridge. Kenyon, too, had a stroke of luck then for, when Sven-Göran Eriksson went to see him in his London flat, a newspaper photographer's prying lens was trained on the semi-transparent curtains. Once Kenyon and Eriksson had been caught together, the Football Association had a clear duty. Or so many of us thought. But, instead of indicating to the country that they could hardly afford to stand in the Swede's way, they gave Eriksson a cuddle and pay rise and Kenyon had to look elsewhere.

He now looked in the obvious place: the Champions League, where the 41-year-old Mourinho and the even younger Didier Deschamps, whose Monaco were to knock Chelsea out of the competition in the semi-final, were working their wonders on limited resources. He went for Mourinho, who, from then on, began working his wonders on unlimited resources. First Mourinho talked a good game. Then his Chelsea team played one. His implicit promise of the earth was about to be delivered. Just as it had been at Porto. He was doing what it said on the tin marked 'special'.

Why else did we like him as we shopped for Christmas in 2004? Many Arsenal supporters felt they had reason to thank him because he kept putting one over on Sir Alex Ferguson. At the same time there were United fans who simply liked the fact that he was not Arsène Wenger. Neutrals were grateful for a disturbance of the none-too-cosy duopoly that had ruled English football for twelve years with scarcely an interruption. They thought Mourinho might spice up the so-called mind games between Ferguson and Wenger, which were getting tedious in a way all fans of television soap opera would have found familiar. There were other factors in his popularity, including his looks – I mean: lots of people have a nice smile, and Mourinho's would melt ice, but he even has a nice scowl – and that indefinable quality which inspires curiosity. Why, I remember people asking at Christmas parties, does such a dapper man not shave before being interviewed on television after matches? Why does he leave his tie slightly loose?

So much for the tittle-tattle of a celebrity-obsessed age. Mourinho had also been disarming his fellow coaches, the faces of the English footballing establishment, who had called him arrogant when he first came but who now grinned when you uttered his name and spoke with an affection not normally accorded the ridiculously advantaged. 'His team became so good so quickly,' said David Moyes, 'that you just had to admire him. He instilled such confidence and belief in his team and, while that's easier when you have top players, he did it at Porto too. So you could see that he'd earned his stripes, come up through the ranks and deserved to be in this top job.' All over the country coaches warmed to Mourinho, albeit with an air of slight bemusement; they noted aspects of his methods while admitting that the whole package defied analysis because he kept getting so much right and so little wrong. Even Ferguson and Wenger had their recurrent weaknesses; neither, to take a common instance, appeared capable of distinguishing a top-class goalkeeper from a cheese-and-tomato sandwich (at least until Ferguson belatedly hit upon the idea of bringing

Edwin van der Sar from Fulham). Mourinho, having resuscitated the career of Vítor Baía at Porto, arrived at Chelsea at the same time as the best keeper from the 2004 European Championship, Petr Čech, and, after initially deciding to start the season with the man in possession, the much-respected Carlo Cudicini, had a late change of mind on the evidence of pre-season performances and promoted the newcomer; before long, Čech was to set a Premier League record by going 1,025 minutes without conceding a goal.

Underneath it all, I suppose, we were still waiting for Mourinho to fall. Not maliciously but out of curiosity. To see if the tin split. To discover what was inside it.

Blippin' marvellous

So after the Christmas of 2004 was past and people, having given with enormous generosity to tsunami-relief funds, returned to life's trivia, the occasional threat to Mourinho's status in our football-oriented society arose.

Towards the end of January it was reported that Mourinho, with Kenyon and two agents – so hazardous had football's waters become, it appeared, that even the agents were going around in pairs – had gathered in a London hotel room with Ashley Cole. The Arsenal and England left-back had two and a half years left on his club contract at the time and was therefore not allowed, under Premier League regulations, to meet a prospective new employer without permission from his current bosses: 'tapped', as the vernacular would have it. Arsenal clearly did not want to lose one of the more important members of Arsène Wenger's squad and were acutely displeased. Mourinho tried to dance out of discomfort, quipping that he had been in Milan on the day in question with Adriano (Internazionale's Brazilian striker, with whom, we were left to presume, Mourinho had been linked by the Italian press), but the joke fell flat on its face.

A few days later, Chelsea's doctor, Neil Frazer, left the club. Although the reason was officially given as ill health, he had incurred Mourinho's displeasure on several occasions.

Then the Cole allegation was revisited, the *Sun* producing a witness, a 24-year-old room-service waiter called Ray Mason, a fine specimen of a breed unique to the English tabloid landscape in that he spoke almost entirely in fluent journalese. Mourinho, Mason claimed, had been rude to him, waving him away without a word when he tried to lay a plate. 'It wasn't until later,' Mason added, 'that I realised the enormity of what I had seen – a dodgy meeting that could blow the Premier League race wide open.' He alluded to Chelsea's substantial lead in the race, the implication being that, if the Premier League were to dock points from Chelsea as a punishment, Manchester United and Arsenal might be allowed back into serious contention for the title. However, although the Premier League appointed a retired judge to conduct an inquiry into the affair, no one acquainted with the politics and practice of football was ever in the slightest doubt that Chelsea would receive a fine, which turned out to be £300,000, and a warning in the form of a three-point deduction, suspended for a year. Mourinho was fined £200,000 and later appealed; Cole was relieved of £100,000.

Their crime, in truth, was to be found out; most clubs 'tap' prospective signings in one way or another, usually through an intermediary, who might be an agent, a fellow player or even a journalist. And what, pray, had Kenyon been doing with Eriksson that night when the snooping snapper caught them through the curtains? The Football Association saw no value in an inquiry into their own employee's behaviour. This Premier League stance smacked of government by show trial. In any case, Chelsea dropped their publicly supposed interest in Cole with alacrity.

One of the agents, Pini Zahavi, had been doing much of their business since Roman Abramovich took over (the other present in the hotel, Jonathan Barnett, was Cole's man). And Zahavi was to figure in another significant episode when, two months after the Cole affair came to light, the ubiquitous Kenyon was found to have hobnobbed in London restaurants one Saturday night with Manchester United's Rio Ferdinand – another client of Zahavi, who was also there. Ferguson seethed and Wenger tartly observed that it was 'like seeing the same movie twice'. Except that Mourinho was now at a distance from the villain's role. While Kenyon protested his innocence, Zahavi stressed that Ferdinand was anxious to stay at United – if only his salary of £70,000 a week could be raised to something more like £120,000

– without dispelling Sir Alex Ferguson's suspicion that his heart was already moving south. Kenyon tried to wipe the fresh mud off his sharp suit. None had stuck to Mourinho. Cole was later to join him at Chelsea.

Of rather more pressing significance, however, were events on boggy fields during the long, wet remainder of this winter of 2004–05. We had been waiting for Chelsea to encounter some adversity. The majority of people were not especially anxious that their Premier League lead be damaged – the most likely challengers, after all, seemed to be Manchester United, for whom little love was to be found outside their own vast global family – but we had a curiosity about how Mourinho and his charges would deal with it. The word most frequently used was 'blip', which was appropriate because Chelsea had been winning with the monotonous regularity of a healthy heartbeat, and the prelude to the week beginning on Sunday, 20 February featured much speculation that this might be the time. Mourinho duly announced he would send a weakened team to Newcastle for the FA Cup tie on that day, explaining that his key players – the likes of John Terry, Frank Lampard and Damien Duff – were not 'Supermen' and would have to be rested in readiness for the even more important Champions League first leg in Barcelona three days later.

Given that the week or, to be precise, period of eight days was to culminate in a Carling Cup final against Liverpool in Cardiff that would present Chelsea with an opportunity to take their first trophy under Mourinho, many felt he had little option but to rotate his players. He chose to blame the FA for making Chelsea play so late in the weekend prior to a Champions League week (and had a point, for all the Spanish and Italian contenders for Europe's biggest prize, including Barcelona, had finished their domestic matches by Saturday night), but it was a useful test for his expensively assembled reserves and they failed it. With Chelsea a goal down at half-time in the Tyneside sleet – the conditions were so inclement Mourinho had abandoned his customary grey cashmere coat for something more suited to a ski slope – he gambled by sending on all three of his permitted substitutes in the shapes of Lampard, Duff and Eidur Gudjohnsen. Within a few minutes Wayne Bridge had been carried off with a broken ankle. Chelsea, unable to equalise despite an improved level of performance, lost another man when their goalkeeper, on this occasion Carlo Cudicini, was sent off, leaving them with nine players, two of whom, Duff and William Gallas, were limping as a result of collisions and rated doubtful to start at Barcelona.

In the previous match, a Premier League visit to Everton, the home side had been reduced to ten men early when James Beattie foolishly butted Gallas, helping Chelsea to overcome an obstacle that was expected to be one of their more difficult on the road to the title. Mourinho, when it was put to him that Sir Alex Ferguson had cited this as an example of luck, replied, in a tone that affected surprise: 'No. I don't feel that. Because Beattie made a big mistake. He deserved a red card. If he had not deserved a red card and the referee showed him one, yes, I'd say the luck was with me.' This kind of logic, upon which, in my experience, every single successful coach is able to call at will, demands a great deal of thought from us. Could it now, I wondered, be applied to Mourinho's misfortune? Had he suddenly become, to paraphrase Napoleon, an unlucky general? Or, even worse, had he unnecessarily exposed players to injury with a mad gamble that would leave them debilitated in Barcelona and, perhaps, Cardiff?

Whatever the truth of the matter, we looked to the bench for a slippage of composure. We saw Mourinho congratulate his Newcastle counterpart, Graeme Souness, a few seconds before the final whistle and then, having walked on to the pitch, first console his own players then shake hands with several of their conquerors. He had performed this last act of sportsmanship before, but never, surely, in such circumstances. Interviewed afterwards, he said he was proud of his players, tendered a compliment to the referee, Mark Halsey, and added that he hoped Newcastle would continue to progress to the FA Cup final.

Such dignity was not only inherently pleasant but efficacious in applying a bandage to Chelsea's wound, and it occurred to me that Arsène Wenger could have done with a touch of the same at Old Trafford earlier in the season. There, Arsenal were put out of their stride, and deprived of the distinction of having gone fifty League matches unbeaten, by Manchester United's unedifyingly harsh tackling – to be precise, that of the Neville brothers on José Antonio Reyes – and a couple of refereeing decisions. The so-called Battle of the Buffet ensued, during which at least one Arsenal player threw food at Ferguson and the managers became embroiled in a furious confrontation. Arsenal's season was never quite the same again. Not for a few months anyway. It was still pretty good by the standards of most clubs, but soon they began to lose their grip on the Premier League title and had to be content with a fortuitous victory over United in the FA Cup final. Was this because Wenger had let them be burdened by the baggage of Old Trafford? True, the circumstances were different at Newcastle – Mourinho had no one but himself to blame, no outrage to absorb – but he was certainly not going to let a similar loss of momentum occur if he could avoid it. He would not countenance a turning point. He called upon his principles and looked forward, concentrating on the players who would do duty at Camp Nou.

When the Chelsea party landed in Barcelona, it looked as if Mourinho was in top form. He went to the official press conference the day before the match and, without prompting, said he would announce not only his team – there were gasps, because at this level a coach never shows his hand in advance – but Barcelona's too. And he duly did, throwing in the name of the referee for good measure. The referee's name was Anders Frisk. We were to hear much more of it and this time Mourinho could not evade the mud. But for now the surprise of the assembled media representatives was mixed with amusement at Mourinho's latest antic. As for what the players must have thought of such a bold departure from convention, I was reminded of something the former Newcastle manager Arthur Cox told me, when I came across him reading a biography of Montgomery of Alamein. 'Footballers,' he said, 'are like soldiers. They love their generals to be a bit eccentric, like Cloughie. It gives them something to talk about, binds them.' As for the rest of us, we had been charmed like cobras. We sank into our baskets and wished away the nagging reservations aired by the author of an editorial in the Spanish newspaper *AS*, who had said of Mourinho, after listening to his boast of having won as many European titles in his relatively short time at Porto (one) as Barcelona had done in their entire history: 'Although he won many trophies in Portugal, there were too many bad manners shown to opponents and too many dirty tricks. He has continued that at Chelsea.'

No doubt the author of those sentiments smiled in vindication as Duff, who had not been among the names listed by Mourinho, ran out at the Camp Nou. The explanation that the Irishman's recovery had been quicker than expected was received sceptically. But the fall from grace was only beginning. At half-time, with Chelsea leading 1–0, the teams were heading down the tunnel when the Barcelona coach, Frank Rijkaard, approached Frisk and said he felt Chelsea's goal should have been disallowed for offside against Duff. This was an inaccurate observation made in the wrong way at the wrong time and the Swedish referee told him so. But it was not as wrong as Chelsea's subsequent imputations against Frisk. An allegation that Rijkaard had been witnessed leaving Frisk's room was scorned (even by the English press, who, though they do love a drama, especially if it involves a wily foreign villain or two, also pride themselves on being able to spot a false claim from a mile away). A jaundiced eye also met Mourinho's implication that Frisk had proceeded to favour Barcelona by sending off Didier Drogba, who was shown a second yellow card for having raised his foot in challenging the goalkeeper. Down to ten men again, Chelsea had been unable to stem the flow of Barcelona attacks and lost 2–1.

Now Mourinho was not so cocky. He refused to attend the post-match media conference and instructed his players not to give any interviews either. Meanwhile Chelsea leaked the allegation about Rijkaard and Frisk and promised to lodge an official protest with UEFA, the governing body of European football. Since, from the moment of Mourinho's appointment, Chelsea had been indivisible from his image, it was he who bore the brunt of it. For the first time, he was not being taken seriously.

He had returned to the city where, under Bobby Robson and then Louis van Gaal, he used to work, undoubtedly one of football's capitals, and behaved in a manner that made him appear provincial. His peevish flouncing was a hark back to the great divide between Oporto and Lisbon, which all too often manifests itself in suspicion that a referee has either been bought or is giving the rub of the green free of charge. Mourinho's president during the great revival of Porto, Jorge Nuno Pinto da Costa, encouraged this. It is a far from exclusively Portuguese phenomenon. A similarly paranoid atmosphere has been observed in other small ponds inhabited by big fish: Scotland comes to mind. But there was another plausible reason, which arose in a conversation I had with Van Gaal, why Barcelona should have been the place where Mourinho went too far. Although Mourinho would probably not admit it, he had unfinished business with the Catalan club. For all that his years there gave him the perfect grounding for a top coach, Mourinho was often treated almost dismissively in Barcelona, referred to among the club's large media entourage (and even by some within the club) as 'The Translator'. This may help to explain his otherwise gratuitous-sounding reminder that he had won as many European titles as Barcelona. It may even excuse that. It hardly justified his dragging of Frisk into the crossfire of the ensuing battle.

So the form of defiance Mourinho chose did his reputation no favours and he was to pay for it with banishment from the dugout and dressing rooms during each leg of the next Champions League contest, against Bayern Munich. It could, of course, have been argued on his behalf that the purpose of his post-match behaviour in the Camp Nou had been to deflect attention from the failure of his team to adjust tactically to Drogba's dismissal. If so, it was a ploy in which only a Machiavellian – 'in order to keep his people united and faithful', wrote Machiavelli, 'a prince must not be concerned with being reputed as a cruel man' – would have taken great pride.

Nor did Mourinho distinguish himself on the eighth day. He became the most prominent figure in a cup final, and for a coach to assume that role, as Paul Hayward sharply observed in the *Daily Telegraph*, was about as appropriate as for a referee to do so. It was Sunday, 27 February and Chelsea's opportunity in Cardiff to win the Carling Cup. By overcoming Liverpool at the Millennium Stadium they could lay hands on their first trophy of the epoch and, while gripping that emotionally precious metal, more acutely sense the comforting notion of Mourinho as Midas. Again, however, the coach saw much to ruffle him on the pitch and was animated as his men strove to cancel out a goal which John Arne Riise had quite beautifully struck on the volley in the first minute with the assistance of Chelsea marking loose enough to raise a statue's eyebrows.

A quarter of an hour from what might have been the final whistle came assistance from Steven Gerrard, the

Liverpool captain who had nearly joined Chelsea the previous summer; endeavouring to assist his defence, he headed into his own net. Mourinho rose from the bench and, smirking, put a pointed index finger to his lips, as if to say 'Shush'. A section of Liverpool supporters behind him took offence and Mourinho, on the advice of the fourth official, Phil Crossley, was escorted down the tunnel. He went to the Sky television room, where, in a state of extreme agitation, he watched the thirty minutes of extra time, during which a 3–2 victory was secured. He emerged for the presentation of the trophy and medals and resumed his habit of approaching the players of both sides. After congratulating his men, he toured the dejected Liverpool ranks, coaches, backroom boys and players, including Gerrard, whose hand he clutched and face he sympathetically cupped; Gerrard responded with a pat on the ribcage. Mourinho was enjoying himself hugely and the thought did occur, not for the first time, that here was something that set Mourinho apart from his fellow coaches: while most of them react to the final whistle by making for the dressing rooms, his instincts take him in the opposite direction. Might he, in gravitating towards the pitch, be seeking his share of the limelight he could never attract as a player?

Maybe it is not quite as simple as that. Maybe; he does love footballers as a breed and is genuinely drawn to their presence. But, in essence, the answer is yes. Mourinho is a performer. There is a passage in the book he produced with his journalist friend Luís Lourenço about how, when he returned to Benfica as Porto coach, he milked the abuse of a huge crowd before the match: 'I made a point of walking on alone, before the team ... It was fantastic, an amazing feeling. I had never been a first-class player who could feel, for example, what Figo had felt upon returning to Barcelona [with Real Madrid], and so I had no idea what it would be like to have 80,000 people whistling and jeering at me. I believe that, when we are mentally strong, those people who seek to intimidate and disturb us have exactly the opposite effect. Upon hearing the whistles and jeers ... I felt as if I were the most important person in the world.'

Anyone seeing him amid the more congenial atmosphere of the Millennium Stadium that late afternoon – most of the Liverpool supporters had drifted away, leaving the steep slopes to the hordes of blue-bedecked celebrators – would have thought him a happy man indeed. Yet behind the serenity of his smile was a grievance waiting to emerge and the post-match interviews provided the ideal opportunity. The first questioner to confront him was Sky's pitchside man, Geoff Shreeves, who, after the routine on-camera pleasantries (in which Shreeves inquires as to how big a win it is and the triumphant coach, without being able to quantify it in cubic centimetres, says he is delighted for the club and the supporters), asked Mourinho if he regretted the behaviour that had led to his banishment from the arena. 'I don't regret,' he replied. 'I have a lot of respect for Liverpool fans and the signal was not for them. It was for the English press.' Balderdash. But he had hinted at a problem with journalists before the match, accusing them of increasing the stress of expectation on Chelsea by mentioning the money the club had spent on players. Such bizarre complaints scarcely register with press or public and are, in any case, primarily intended for consumption by the complainant's players as a motivational device. The unusual development here was that Mourinho was also looking for a confrontation with Sky, who are not usually regarded within football as mischievous (and have sound commercial reasons for wanting to maintain that reputation). Addressing Shreeves directly, as if holding the pitchside reporter responsible for every utterance of every commentator and analyst employed by Rupert Murdoch's organisation, he asserted: 'In my opinion you try to do everything to disturb Chelsea.' He had watched Sky's coverage of a Premier League match the previous day, in which Manchester United, by beating Portsmouth, had cut Chelsea's advantage over them to six points. 'You spoke more about Chelsea than Manchester United and, because the gap was cut, the sun shone.' When Shreeves responded that he sounded like a man under pressure, Mourinho flatly denied it.

So much for the dignity he had exuded at Newcastle a week earlier – and for which he had been praised by the Sky presenter Richard Keys. Once again we had seen the

Porto mentality, the belief that the media would take one side or another for sinister reasons rather than, by loose consensus, arrive at the typically English notion – presumably expressed by the commentator at Old Trafford that Saturday when United won – that the result would add interest to the title race.

Often the top coaches are more pleasant in defeat than victory. Arsène Wenger is an exception, but Sir Alex Ferguson could occasionally accept adversity with good grace. The Scot could also turn a moment of vindication into a weapon and that was what Mourinho did in Cardiff. What a week it had been. He had maintained his reputation as a winner despite having encountered the blip, but along the way lost a little of his allure. The fact that he was tucked out of sight while his players were scoring the goals that took the Cup to west London was noted. The *Daily Mirror*, for so long a sorry example of a thing that ain't what it used to be, echoed its glorious past with a picture of the Chelsea players and the headline: 'They won it – he lost it.'

The perception of Mourinho had subtly altered. There were echoes here of what had happened to the England team's first foreign coach. When the FA had appointed Sven-Göran Eriksson in 2000 he was lauded for his calmness and restraint – yet two years later when England slumped to defeat by Brazil in the World Cup, the same 'cool' Swede was criticised for lacking the blood-and-thunder approach we were supposed to have rejected.

Now the new king of cool had lost his crown. Mourinho's honeymoon was over.

Some people thought the 'Shush' gesture innocuous, arguing that if Liverpool fans could not cope with a bit of banter they were in the wrong game. Others thought it ridiculously childish behaviour for someone in a position of leadership. Certainly if a player had done anything exceptionally silly – if Wayne Rooney had scored for Manchester United on his return to Everton, say, then mooned at the crowd and been sent off – he could have expected condemnation on all sides. And, had the hypothetical offender been a Chelsea player, he would surely have been referred to the strict code of conduct every squad member was handed after Mourinho arrived at Stamford Bridge. Later Mourinho was to touch on the issue of what was and was not acceptable, saying he had seen Adriano celebrate with such a gesture after scoring a goal for Inter without upsetting anyone. It was not the first time he had used Adriano to illustrate a point. Nor was it the first time Mourinho had confused himself with a star footballer. But there is a difference, surely, between the standards expected of a coach and a player, just as the teacher is expected to be above the more mischievous traits of the pupil. Critics wondered if such debates might be raging within a polyglot squad. But word came back that the dressing room was solidly behind Mourinho the winner. So the players did not see him as a posturing narcissist.

In the pre-Mourinho period, a prevalent characteristic of top coaches in England was the knack of being able to mask any selfishness in their ambition. Sir Alex Ferguson always gave the impression of being willing to fight for his players if necessary, Arsène Wenger of regarding them almost as his own flesh and blood. Mourinho infuses the players with his own super-confidence, creating an almost evangelical atmosphere. In this sense, he follows in the tradition of Bill Shankly, who made Liverpool's Anfield stadium a fortress in the sixties.

Once, when an inexperienced reporter for the *Guardian* in Manchester, I resolved to interview Shankly by phone. The subject my sports editor had chosen was Ian Callaghan, a midfielder for whom Shankly had an acknowledged and understandable affection. I rang Anfield and asked to be put through to Shankly – these days you would be transferred to a media department which would advise you to come to the manager's weekly briefing or, if that were too late for your purpose, consult the club's website – and the next thing I knew a familiar rasping voice, the sort of voice you would get by crossing James Cagney with a Scottish coal miner, was on the line.

'Yes!'

He had to say it twice because I hesitated, feeling not only unworthy but, to be honest, frightened.

'Mr Shankly?'

'Yes! Yes!'

'Um, Mr Shankly, what do you think of Ian Callaghan?'

There was a silence that seemed to last an eternity before Shankly spoke again. And then he spat it out:

'Jesus Christ!'

I was about to apologise for having troubled him when he continued: 'Aye, son, Jesus Christ.' And I realised he was answering my question. 'Cally's the nearest thing on this earth to Jesus Christ.' The way he lived his life was an example to all; he was gentle and yet courageous; and so it went on, Shankly talking vividly while my heart pounded at the excitement of securing such a dramatic tribute as the introduction to my piece. Shankly had a similar level of admiration for quite a few of his players, among them Kevin Keegan and the late Emlyn Hughes, and never hesitated to express it and, partly in consequence, they felt and behaved like world-beaters.

There was a reminder of this when Mourinho spoke before the trip to Barcelona. In truth, for all Sir Alex Ferguson might have been saying about luck, Chelsea had not been enjoying the best of it. In particular they had lost Arjen Robben through injury – not for the first time and not for the last during a season in which the young Dutchman still demonstrated that, if allowed more opportunities to shine, he might have beaten even Frank Lampard and John Terry to the player-of-the-year awards. Robben had been the victim of a fearsome tackle by Aaron Mokoena at Blackburn and a journalist wondered if Mourinho now wished he had bought a reinforcement in the wide-attacker department during the winter transfer window that had just closed – if only as a temporary measure. Mourinho had stayed out of the market. Was that not taking a risk? Mourinho answered scornfully. 'If I had bought someone for that position,' he said, '*that* would have been a big risk. Because the player I bought could have been on the bench for months. To replace Duff and Robben – no chance! You could buy one of the best players in the world – and he'd end up having to sit on the bench.' It did not answer the question but, as endorsements go, it didn't half ring.

Then Mourinho was asked about his young captain, John Terry, who was having such an inspirational season in the Premier League as to be a hot tip for at least one of the awards (in the event Terry was chosen by the players while Lampard won the football writers' vote). English football was one thing, though, Europe quite another and Barcelona had candidates for world awards. Surely, the next questioner suggested, an attack featuring Ronaldinho and Samuel Eto'o would present a big test of Terry's progress. 'It will be a big test,' replied Mourinho, 'for them.'

Can you imagine how Terry and his team-mates felt when they read their papers the next morning?

Just a few weeks later, however, in the aftermath of their aggregate victory over Bayern Munich in the next round, Mourinho was actually being accused of overshadowing his players' achievements. Under UEFA rules governing the suspension of coaches, he had been banned from having any contact with his players after they arrived at the stadium for each leg. There were the earpiece antics at Stamford Bridge, where he was suspected of transmitting messages by way of a device concealed in the woolly hat of his fitness coach, Rui Faria, and the sudden exit from the stands at Munich's Olympic Stadium when he felt he was being crowded by photographers, journalists and German fans and fled by taxi to the team hotel to watch the match on television. Every day, it seemed, there was a fresh vignette, a new controversy, another reason for Mourinho to hog the headlines. 'I'm not interested in myself,' he insisted. 'I'm not interested in my image and what people think about me, only in getting results. Some of the things I say and do, I'm just thinking of the group. They know me. They understand that.' The players certainly seemed to; they queued to attest that, far from Mourinho's behaviour being a distraction from the pursuit of the biggest prizes, it actually helped them by lightening the pressure.

Meanwhile the method in the apparent madness of his tilting at the UEFA windmill was to make the team feel somehow threatened, cornered and required to stand together against any danger that ensued. To induce the underdog spirit in probably the most financially potent football club the world has ever seen is quite an achievement, but Mourinho's Chelsea never got too comfortable, never went soft, until the battle they most wanted to win, that for the Premier League title, was won.

The enemy of football

Far from being chastened by the widespread revulsion at his comments about the referee in Barcelona, Mourinho told the Portuguese media within a matter of days that the result had been 'adulterated' owing to Frisk's dismissal of Drogba. He was called to account by an irate UEFA and later, after a thrilling Chelsea victory on aggregate at Stamford Bridge had culminated in further rancour – this time the crucial refereeing decision went Mourinho's way as Pierluigi Collina ignored Barcelona's protests that Ricardo Carvalho had illicitly prevented their goalkeeper, Victor Valdés, from reaching John Terry's winning header – Mourinho was ordered to sit out the quarter-final. Coach and club were also fined for the relatively technical offences of having snubbed the press and neglected, despite exhortations, to get their team on the Barcelona pitch in time for the second half to start on schedule. Steve Clarke, one of his assistants, and a security officer, Les Miles, were admonished by UEFA for their parts in the formation of the tale about Rijkaard's visit to the referee's room; Mourinho had since admitted he had seen nothing and relied on the testimony of the pair, whom UEFA deemed guilty of a mere misunderstanding caused by the layout of the stadium.

This is how Mourinho's story lurched ungraciously towards the inevitable, in his own words:

At first: *'When I saw Rijkaard entering the referee's dressing room I couldn't believe it. When Didier Drogba was sent off I wasn't surprised.'*

Several days later: *'Rijkaard was in the referee's room for over five minutes. I know because my assistants were at the door while the meeting took place.'*

And finally, after he had taken refuge in legal advice to go easy on the subject for a while: *'If something happens in a football stadium, and I don't see it, and if some of my people say to me, "I saw this, this happened," and if another one arrives and says, "It's true," I have to believe my people. I have to treat it as the truth, use it as the truth. Because I cannot work without loyalty. I have to believe my people. So, because I'm loyal to my people, I'm involved in something I don't want.'*

Chelsea had been outraged by statements from William Gaillard, then UEFA's head of communications, who had accused them of, among other things, 'using lies as a pre-match tactic ahead of the second leg' with Barcelona. Who can say whether those falsehoods affected Collina's performance at Stamford Bridge? Certainly there were no lingering complaints from Barcelona. But they were out of the Champions League and Mourinho was in disgrace, offering coded explanations to which no one was really listening.

Meanwhile it had become clear that the real victim of the episode would be an innocent party. Frisk had suddenly retired from refereeing at forty-two (the same age as Mourinho), saying that he was 'scared to let my children leave the house' after threats received by post, telephone and email. The Swede, a little too demonstrative in style and blond-streaked in appearance for some tastes but officially rated behind only Collina in the world, rejected appeals to reconsider from, among others, the chairman of the UEFA referees' committee, Volker Roth, who expressed his revulsion by declaring: 'People like Mourinho are the enemy of football.' Roth was right in the sense that coaches who casually make the referee's lot more onerous and stressful are sabotaging the chances of good decisions; Frisk did say the reason he was leaving the game was that he could no longer trust himself, by which he clearly meant guarantee the purity of his decision-making. But mostly there was just basic human sympathy for him. As the Swiss referee Urs Meier, who had been a victim of similarly vile English threats after denying Sven-Göran Eriksson's national team a goal against Portugal in the European Championship eight months earlier, put it, rather mildly: 'UEFA and FIFA [the world body] have to protect referees from attacks like this.'

A certain disaffection with Chelsea had set in. They were portrayed as an arrogant, bullying club with *nouveau riche* values. Arsène Wenger made a fair point when he asked why Abramovich did not come out and show some leadership – 'I'd like to hear a voice at Chelsea say what they really want to do, what they want to be in England and how they want to behave' – but there was no response and so Mourinho continued to take most of the criticism. The newspapers gave it, energetically and, at times, hysterically, publishing lists of supposed misdemeanours that soon became risible, with anything remotely connected with a difference of opinion being laid at Mourinho's door. One supposed diary of disgrace actually began:

12 Sept., 2004: *Accuses referee Rob Styles of being 'ridiculous' after he fails to give Didier Drogba a penalty in the 0–0 draw at Aston Villa.*

Well, well. A coach is not enamoured of a referee's judgement. Whatever next? In fact, television had proved Mourinho right. But the list went on.

29 Sept.: *Is spat at by Porto fan before Chelsea's 3–1 win at Stamford Bridge in the Champions League.*

Mourinho's part in this crime – provoking the fan by his presence, perhaps – was not described. Nor was it explained why the next charge on the sheet, that of being accused by Adrian Mutu of lying during the Romanian forward's period of serious cocaine abuse, had stuck.

Coincidentally a couple of charges were brought by the FA which must have vexed Mourinho. First Chelsea were fined £15,000 for 'failing to control their players' at Blackburn, where the home side's robust approach had cost Chelsea the services of Arjen Robben. Then Mourinho himself was relieved of £5,000 for having observed of Manchester United's performance in a Carling Cup semi-final: 'In the second half it was whistle and whistle and whistle, fault and fault, cheat and cheat.' The FA should have known that Mourinho was not really calling United cheats. When using the word 'fault', by which he meant 'foul', in conjunction with 'cheat', he was talking about tactical fouling, which, whether we like it or not, is part of the game and should be a legitimate subject of discussion. No wonder, after all the fuss Celtic and Manchester United had made about Porto's little tricks when he had charge of that club, he was angry about these fines. But he was getting to know our ways and the finer nuances of our footballing vocabulary: to refer to an opponent's 'cheating' had become politically incorrect. Except, of course, in relation to foreigners (defined as non-English players who made their living outside the Premier League) such as Deco before he joined Chelsea for a spell.

The Frisk affair was more significant in any language, and although, as Chelsea went into the last month of the season, Mourinho admitted he had made mistakes

– 'it is not necessary to fight every day' – he continued to betray no hint of sympathy for the referee. He even made a joke about Frisk on Portuguese television that verged on the callous. Asked to comment on Porto's 2–0 defeat by Sporting Lisbon, during which his former club had had two players sent off, Mourinho smiled and replied: 'I have to be very careful when I talk about referees because Mr Joao Ferreira may also quit refereeing.' Clearly Frisk's retirement was not weighing too heavily on his conscience.

It was, then, very much in a spirit of defiance that Mourinho approached the visit of Bayern to Stamford Bridge. He even took the opportunity to play mind games with his own employers and Chelsea's first weekend of April, though it included a victory at Southampton, was utterly dominated by reports of how Kenyon and, of course, Abramovich had been made aware that he was (a) not very happy with the standard of support the club had given him during the rows with UEFA, who had themselves privately complained about the attitude of at least one Chelsea employee involved, and (b) not wholly against the notion of a contract extension on highly favourable terms. The contract question had been under discussion for some time but Mourinho's standing had become so high that he had only to cough for everyone at Chelsea to catch a cold – everyone, but everyone, at that time – and so at Peter Kenyon's suggestion Abramovich flew in to meet Mourinho and his agent, Jorge Mendes.

Suddenly all was sweetness and light and the only argument to be heard was between journalists on the question of how much Mourinho's next contract would be worth. A basic £5.2 million a year – a rise of £1 million, presumably – was the lowest estimate. The highest was £9 million, including bonuses and image rights.

Mourinho watched his team beat Bayern 4–2 on television in the fitness centre of the Chelsea Village Hotel, less than a hundred yards from the pitch, and throughout the match events on the bench engaged the media almost as frequently as the excellence of Frank Lampard, who scored one very good goal and one, featuring a chest-trap, turn and half-volley, all in the same smooth movement, that was quite sumptuous, of balletic elegance. Meanwhile Rui Faria, the fitness coach, kept fiddling with the area around his right ear, inducing a suspicion that Mourinho was passing messages to his assistants by telephone, as he had boasted of doing when with Porto. Every now and again a note would be scribbled and handed to Clarke or Mourinho's most senior assistant, Baltemar Brito. Once again Chelsea's players were struggling for space on the back pages the next morning – against their own manager, who had not even been in the stadium. It was becoming more and more difficult to accept what he had said after Cardiff: 'I'm not interested in my image ... I'm just thinking of the group. They know me, they understand that.'

It ought to be added, in fairness to Mourinho, that

the antics of his sidekicks were clearly for the benefit of the players rather than the media. Anyway, insisted Rui Faria, when he turned up in Munich as Mourinho's spokesman at the pre-match press conference: 'I did not have anything under my hat last week and people worry about too many silly things.' Just to be sure, UEFA officials went to him at half-time and ordered him to remove his hat; nothing was found. As an example of closing the stable door after the horse had bolted, this was unbeatable. Chelsea came through the match more comfortably than the 6–5 aggregate score might suggest, earning a semi-final against Liverpool which, given the mutual respect that then existed between Mourinho and his counterpart Rafael Benítez, was bound to pulsate in a vigorous but relatively civilised and adult manner.

Liverpool's supporters played their part. Shortly before the first leg at Stamford Bridge, a scoreless stale-mate, Mourinho left his players and staff in the dressing room and strode deep in thought to the bench to sit alone, as was his custom. He may have forgotten that the area next to the bench at Chelsea is allocated to visit-ing fans. At any rate, he was soon approached by several Liverpudlians making 'Shush' gestures. Mourinho, grin-ning broadly, gave them the thumbs-up before posing for a mobile-phone photograph.

The match was played in a similar spirit and at the end of a deafening second leg, decided in Liverpool's favour by the decision of the Slovakian referee Luboš Michel to award a goal to Luis García in the opening minutes, Mourinho paid tribute to the crowd's influence. There was a double edge to his remarks, for he went on to claim that William Gallas had cleared the ball before the whole of it had crossed the line and blamed one of Michel's linesmen, Roman Slyško, for having signalled a goal; the official, he implied, had been swayed by the Anfield atmosphere. While a body of opinion, fortified by Sky computer images, sympathised with him on this, others pointed out that, if Michel and Slyško had been of a mind to apply the letter of the law rigorously against Chelsea, the referee could have given a penalty against Petr Čech, who had bowled over Milan Baroš seconds earlier, and shown the goalkeeper the red card, leaving Mourinho's team with ten men for almost the whole match.

Anyway, Liverpool and their fevered supporters deserved to reach a final they were destined to win dramatically, even if Mourinho, in asserting afterwards that the better team had lost on this occasion, was unable to resist the temptation to allude to the truth as demonstrated by the Premier League table.

Chelsea went very close to punching their weight. In the sixth and last minute of time added for stoppages, Eidur Gudjohnsen put wide the sort of chance you would expect him to take. But if Chelsea had prevailed, it would have been nothing to do with Mourinho's powers, to which Liverpool, under the more restrained but undoubtedly crafty Benítez, seemed impervious. While spectators, their veins bulging, roared and screamed, the technical area marked out in front of the dugouts staged an oddly dignified play within a play. At one stage Benítez and Mourinho, coincidentally running out to the boundary line to signal instructions to their players, bumped into each other; each briefly smiled, half-turned inwards and raised his arms in a symmetrical gesture of apology. Towards the end of the match, Mourinho became a still, small figure who had run out of ideas and accepted tactical defeat; he had thrown on the beefy young German defender Robert Huth as an additional striker, a ploy hardly calculated to furrow the brows of Sami Hyypia and the outstanding Jamie Carragher. After the final whistle, he went to his players. There were hugs for Terry and Lampard and a special squeeze for the freshly frustrated Gudjohnsen, and then handshakes for the jubilant Liverpool side were followed by applause for the crowd from Mourinho as he disappeared down the tunnel.

Would he now shush? A likely scenario! His complaints about Slyško were made without any reference to the decisions that had worked in his team's favour when Porto survived at Manchester United the previous season and Chelsea triumphed over Barcelona; selective myopia is a widespread affliction among coaches. Whether he chose his words carefully only he can know, but he stopped short of inviting a UEFA charge before, for some reason, reiterating his belief in God and promising that his planning for the next season would start right away.

The principal objective for the current season had been attained only seventy-three hours earlier – Mourinho was still complaining that the Premier League fixture schedule worked against Chelsea's interests in Europe – when they secured the English title at Bolton, two goals from Frank Lampard causing a limited celebration. When Mourinho spotted the players taking an odd swig from the champagne bottles they had been using to spray each other, he 'got the hump' according to a grinning Lampard, and told them to remember Anfield. But he was as happy and fulfilled as anyone else. A few weeks earlier, Mourinho had vouchsafed: 'I predicted at the start of the season that we would win the title in April.' It was 30 April and Mourinho's men were hugging each other. To quote the slogan more precisely: he had done *exactly* what it said on the tin.

The work still to be done meant he could not keep a pledge to stand back once the title was safe, 'to disappear a little bit and let the players enjoy themselves and be the face of our success'. Some hope! The day after Chelsea took the title, a BBC website offering the public 'shares' in sports personalities priced in accordance with the newspaper column inches devoted to them – Mourinho had for some months been the most expensive – showed him at £132.04. You could have Lampard at £16.54 and Terry at £10.77. Wayne Rooney shares were the second priciest at £22.58. So the option of relative obscurity was not open to Mourinho. But, in brief deference to his promise, he was more restrained at Bolton than on other occasions and an indelible image of that warm evening at the Reebok Stadium is of him alone in the dugout with his mobile phone and the loveliest, most relaxed smile, one that exuded pure pleasure rather than the triumphalism normally evident on these occasions. When he had finished, the Sky interviewer Geoff Shreeves went over and asked who the conversation had been with and he replied: 'My wife, my kids.' It was difficult to believe that this was the belligerent blusterer of Barcelona, the carping curmudgeon of Cardiff, but they were all one and the same. We had before us a much more complicated character than Mourinho's initial conquest of the English game's affections may have suggested.

When I asked Sir Bobby Robson if Mourinho had rubbed people up the wrong way in Portugal or Spain as he had done since coming to England, he answered: 'No, never. Not in our time together anyway.' So he, Robson, had never seen the strutting figure who taunted the Liverpool supporters in Cardiff? 'No, not really.' So what had changed him – fame? 'Well,' said Robson, 'let me tell you. And it's happened to me. It happens to all of us. We acquire a bit of power, don't we? Through success. You get a bit of power. You know what you stand for. You know what people think of you. And this power, this control you have over people, becomes ingrained into you. You develop a stronger personality. Look at Brian

Clough and the way he developed. At one time Cloughie wasn't the Old Big 'Ead he became. He always had visions that he might get that way, probably, but he had to behave in a certain manner. All successful managers, if you look at them, have that strength of personality. You use your position to be powerful. More powerful than you basically are.'

The notion of Mourinho as a victim of the syndrome, a managerial megalomaniac, was seductive; after all, he became accustomed to dominance at Porto, and now he had the purse of one of the world's richest men with which to build an empire. But Robson's great friend Gérard Houllier thought the motivation was more likely to be a desire for revenge than power. 'I can imagine he'd had a lot of abuse at the Millennium Stadium,' the former Liverpool coach continued, 'because Chelsea had been 1–0 down for a long time. So he was saying to them, "You've had a go at me – now be quiet." Like players do.' But he is not a player and the difference was outlined by William Gaillard, the UEFA official who so irked Chelsea when, while accepting that Mourinho had not intended to whip up such serious malice as Anders Frisk was made to suffer, he said: 'Coaches are role models for players and fans. They have a duty to behave better than anyone else.' Was that not the case? Houllier nodded. So had Mourinho not gone too far in Barcelona? 'Yes, but it's easy to say that sitting in a comfortable chair in a quiet room when there's no crowd in your ears and things going on. In our job, we sometimes get a bit paranoid.'

Quite so. And when I told Houllier what I have seen it do to the most civilised and intelligent of them – notably induce the emission of utter twaddle, especially on the subject of referees – he gave a chuckle of recognition. 'I know – even Arsène!' Neither Wenger nor Houllier has been known to tell a crowd to shut up. But Wenger on occasion has defended the indefensible and Houllier seethed against referees. 'I think,' said Houllier, 'that, when things don't go your way, you are trying to rationalise, to find an explanation, and sometimes that leads you down the wrong road. Now I have gone back into management I hope I'll be different, because I've been on the other side, working for French television, and can see the futility of how we sometimes behave. It's incredible. I never saw it before. I can see now that even José Mourinho gives too much importance to certain things. But in his place, a few years ago, I'd have felt no differently. And what we have to remember is that, despite the brilliance of José's career, he is still in the early stages of it.' Houllier then offered the following hostage to fortune: 'the more he wins the more humble he will get. He is a rough diamond who will gradually become smoother and better, both as a coach and as a man.'

It did seem to happen with Houllier. When he spoke about Mourinho, he was back in France, with Olympique Lyonnais. He went on to resume work with the national federation before returning to England to join Aston

Villa in 2010. There, Houllier did seem a lighter, calmer man. And Mourinho? We waited to see. It had happened to Brian Clough, who, though alcoholism began to sap his strength when he was not much older than Mourinho when he joined Chelsea, became one of the most principled of managers; when Clough died, past referees lined up to form a metaphorical guard of honour, for his teams had been models of discipline. Whether Mourinho will ever bring to his manipulative skills such an unashamedly moral dimension remains to be judged.

Yet during a break in Chelsea's 2004–05 season there was evidence that he valued things other than the pursuit of victory. At the end of March, when his players dispersed to join their various national squads for World Cup qualifying matches, Mourinho flew to Israel. He had been approached two months earlier by the Peres Center for Peace and asked for help in drawing worldwide attention to a programme designed to foster peace by bringing together Israeli and Palestinian children to play football in mixed teams. Mourinho readily agreed and the commitment he displayed during a three-day visit impressed every observer. With Shimon Peres, the deputy prime minister, he mingled with countless children and one day he gave a lecture to around 250 Israeli and Palestinian coaches, complete with visual projections he had clearly taken the trouble to prepare himself, drawing on experience; Mourinho was a teacher for three years before he went into football full-time. The odd instance of semantic originality – 'improvisibility' was one concept that lost something in translation – only added to the charm. Even hard-to-impress journalists were enthralled. 'When it was over,' one told me, 'I looked at my watch and he'd been speaking for an hour and thirty-five minutes. The time had flashed by.'

Another writer who went on the trip, Matt Hughes, then of the London *Evening Standard*, wrote that, when Mourinho stood back in his white T-shirt to address an enlarged photograph of himself and Frank Lampard locked in an embrace after the Carling Cup final, he went all sensitive, as if sharing his wedding pictures with the audience. 'This,' Mourinho told the coaches, 'looks like a hug, but it's more than a hug … this is a hug that shows we trust each other. Without words he's saying to me "Thanks" and I'm saying to him "Thanks". This is a hug that we repeat player after player because we are a family.'

Upon reading that, I thought about Adrian Mutu, the player thrown out of the Chelsea family for taking cocaine. Then I reflected that there can be a limit to any parent's patience. It is natural, sometimes, when you listen to the puffed-up figures of a coach's speech, to think: bullshit. But Mutu, like every player on the Chelsea staff at the start of the 2004–05 season, was told Mourinho wanted only players willing to gear everything, including their social lives, to the demands of success. The Romanian broke his implicit promise and, after ignoring warnings, had to be punished for it. But at the end of every moral discussion surrounding Mourinho you came back to the same question: what had the family of Anders Frisk done to offend him? Football, for all the light it might occasionally bring into the lives of the children of the Gaza Strip, can be a nasty business.

Mourinho, according to Chelsea's *bête noire*, William Gaillard of UEFA, had brought 'a lot of new things to football, many of them positive', but he had to remember he was in a position of responsibility. The trouble with being a top-level coach, however, is that it involves such a lot of acting. And how can a man be sure what his position is when briefly – in the interests of the team, of course – he has forgotten who *he* is. Coaches are often ham actors, playing to the gallery or the media, sometimes with a different act for each. José Mourinho was unusual; he was like a one-man show in which he played a wide variety of roles. He could do a passable megalomaniac, or be paranoid. He could strut in full of bombast, nakedly adversarial, ready to take on the world. Or he could be vulnerable; often, when he was in this frame of mind, a shark metaphor was just around the corner (understandably enough, given that he was brought up so near the Portuguese coast). At the height of his conflict with UEFA and Barcelona, he mused: 'I feel like a boy swimming between sharks.' When there was a lull, you came to expect a storm, and the other way round. And yet he always seemed to surprise us, to hold our attention and keep us guessing, just as those of a certain age could remember Clough being able to. There had been articles in the broadsheets discussing the connection between madness and genius (or at least eccentricity and being an outstanding football manager) which you could well have imagined adorning the colour supplements in Clough's day. Clough liked to swing from mood to mood. He would portray himself as a dictator one day, a caring socialist the next – in 1973 he was described by Malcolm Allison, another of the more flamboyant managers, as 'a kind of Rolls-Royce communist'.

Most managers have tended to specialise in a certain kind of role. George Graham, who guided Arsenal to the English championship in 1989 and 1991, was always pleased to be considered a strict disciplinarian. He played up to it and, even though there was usually a slight twinkle in his eye, it was seldom noticed. Yet during his time in charge the club's disciplinary record off the field left a lot to be desired. Tony Adams, before he began his inspiring recovery from alcoholism, even served a term of imprisonment for a driving offence which could only be described as extreme. As for Arsenal's on-the-field reputation, suffice it to say that in the glorious season of 1990–91, when they lost but a single match in the League (to Chelsea), the only other people to take more than a point out of a meeting with them were the FA, who docked two as a punishment for their part in a twenty-one-man brawl at Old Trafford (Alex Ferguson's

Manchester United had one point deducted). There was one very disciplined aspect of Graham's Arsenal: the defence. So maybe he will always be reviewed in the stern image of his back four. Nor will Graham – in real life, always one of the most pleasant and approachable men in the managerial game – mind going down in history as, if not quite football's answer to Captain Bligh of the *Bounty*, a man who liked nothing more than to run a tight ship.

I sometimes think these people are having fun at our expense; I really do. There was often a whimsical air about Clough that suggested he could see through football and the people in it. Maybe one day Mourinho will reach that stage. But at Chelsea he was very different, all but admitting he could tailor his mood to suit what he judged to be his team's requirements at any given time. It was, however, surely fair to scrutinise the theory that, as he put it eight days before the first Premier League title had been claimed: 'While I have been fighting every day, there has been calm around the team.' Does it actually calm a player when his boss is marched down the Millennium Stadium tunnel with half an hour of a cup final to go and the score 1–1? If that were a sight guaranteed to improve a team's performance, every coach would be trying to get himself collared. True, the vast montage of newspaper headlines that turned nine months of Mourinho's professional life into the first series of a soap opera must have lightened the mood at Chelsea's training ground, where everyone exuded confidence in the knowledge that they could tell where the act ended and Mourinho their friend and leader began. Mourinho alluded to this when, on the eve of the Champions League visit to Anfield, he said: 'I'm not selfish. I'm not the man some people think I am. Only the players really know what and who I am.' But, for the rest of us, the task of working out a little of Mourinho and analysing why he chose to do things in the way he did was tricky.

He was an exceptionally gifted psychologist – that much was clear – and a great deal besides. Which is what they used to say about Carl Gustav Jung, the original differentiator between extrovert and introvert personalities. My wild guess would be that Mourinho is, was and always had been an extrovert. But, if we are to discover a bit more, we might as well begin, as the real analysts do, with the child.

PART THREE

The formative years

Born into football

On 26 January 1963, John F. Kennedy was president of the United States. He had less than a year to live; it was the 700th of the 1,000 days that culminated in his assassination. Harold Macmillan was Britain's prime minister and that morning he would have noted the West German cabinet's unanimous declaration of support for British entry into the Common Market, which was to grow into the European Union. The notion of Portuguese membership of the Common Market would have been almost laughable because, quite apart from its relative poverty, Portugal had been a dictatorship since 1926. Although outwardly tranquil enough, it still harboured a widespread fear of António Salazar's political police, the Polícia Internacional de Defesa do Estado, or PIDE.

So much for the political situation. Now for the sport and weather. So deep was this British midwinter that all but eight ties in the fourth round of the FA Cup were postponed and Chelsea flew to Malta to escape the freeze. On 26 January, they played a local select team in Valletta. Meanwhile in Portugal the game went on, dominated by the Benfica of Eusébio, Mário Coluna and José Águas, who had been champions of Europe in each of the previous two seasons (and were to reach the final again that year, only to lose to Milan at Wembley). Benfica were not only respected throughout Europe for their marvellously skilful football but considered rather exotic because, unusually among European sides at that time, they had black players. These had come from the African colonies: Eusébio and Coluna were from Mozambique, Joaquim Santana from Angola. On 26 January, the great Eusébio and his team-mates were engaged in the recovery of the national title from their Lisbon rivals Sporting (they were to win it by a substantial margin). And in the port of Setúbal, just twenty miles south of Lisbon, where the Sado river joins the Atlantic, the creature eventually to be known throughout the world as José Mourinho was born.

His full name was José Mário dos Santos Mourinho Félix. His father was Félix Mourinho, a professional footballer, a goalkeeper who was to represent Portugal, albeit only once and very, very briefly. Indeed so short was Félix Mourinho's international career to be that, if you had put an egg on to boil as it started, you would only just have turned off the gas, spooned the egg from the pan and cracked the thing open when it ended. It lasted from the eighty-second minute of a match against the Republic of Ireland in Recife, Brazil, until the final whistle. Yes, Félix Mourinho had a mere eight minutes in his country's service, as a substitute for José Henrique. At least he kept a clean sheet. Portugal were leading the Irish 2–1 when he came on and it stayed that way.

You may wonder what the Portuguese and Irish squads were doing on the north-east coast of Brazil. They had been invited by the host nation to take part in a tournament called the Independence Cup in the summer of 1972. Brazil won it, beating Portugal 1–0 in the final, which was no surprise because two years earlier the Brazilians had lifted the World Cup by the abundant virtue of a team some judges still consider the finest in football's entire history: Pelé, Jairzinho, Rivelino and Gérson were among its stars. Portugal's star of stars, Eusébio, could probably have done without the Independence Cup. He was over thirty and years of brutal tackling had taken a toll on his legs. 'I was instructed to do a man-to-man marking job on him,' Mick Martin recalled. Martin, later to begin a career in England with Manchester United, was at that time a spindly twenty-one-year-old part-timer running a Dublin sports shop. 'I felt I kept the great man pretty quiet,' he said. 'I'm serious – our manager, Liam Tuohy, told me that too.' Félix Mourinho, like Mick Martin, would always remember 25 June 1972. But first he would go home and tell his family about it. Especially his son. His nine-year-old son José.

Félix Mourinho had long been acknowledged in

Portugal as a proficient last line of defence and had made a more than respectable career with Vitória of Setúbal and later Lisbon's third force, Belenenses, for whom he was playing at the age of thirty-five when he went to the tournament in Brazil.

Young José and his sister Teresa, four years his elder, had a comfortable start in life. They grew up among an extended family in a large house on the estate of their wealthy great-uncle, Mário Ascensao Ledo, the owner of sardine canneries in not only Setúbal but Oporto and the Algarve, whose beneficence had included the donation of land and money for the building of the Vitória club's Bonfim Stadium. Both materially and emotionally, José was well looked after. He attended a private school and, when he came home, there were trees to provide shade in the garden, where he played football, sometimes with his father and sometimes with one of the family's servants, an elderly man; in addition there were two maids. His father also took him horse-riding. 'Although José was always small,' an aunt said, 'he had no fear.' But most of his spare moments were devoted to football. Either playing or watching his father train; Félix loved to take José to work and clearly intended to give the boy every chance of following in his footsteps to the professional ranks. José's mother, Maria Júlia Mourinho (née Ledo), was a primary-school teacher whose spare time would often be spent on church activities. A devout Catholic with a strong personality, she made sure José attended

Rebel with a cause: according to Desmond Morris, the ideal actor to play Mourinho would be James Dean (*Coloursport*).

All together now: a feature of the Mourinho regime is the *bonhomie* between players and staff, here exuded by Damien Duff, Frank Lampard and Mourinho (*Getty Images*).

Mourinho's father, Felix (*above left*), was the first to recognise and nurture his talent as a coach. Later José continued his education with Sir Bobby Robson, who took him to Barcelona to work with great players such as Ronaldo – here helping Robson to show off the European Cup Winners' Cup – and Louis Van Gaal. The Dutchman broadened Mourinho's experience by allowing him to take charge of the team from time to time (*Empics & Coloursport*).

The special ones: Mourinho with the Champions League trophy after Porto's triumph over Monaco in May 2004 and, just five weeks later, at Chelsea with his closest aides (from left): fitness coach Rui Faria, scout André Villas Boas, goalkeeper coach Silvino Louro and assistants Stevie Clarke and Baltemar Brito (*Empics & AFP/Getty Images*).

A man for all seasons: Mourinho and Newcastle assistant Dean Saunders watch through the sleet as Chelsea go out of the FA Cup at St James' Park. In the warmer conditions offered by Tel Aviv, Mourinho addresses Israeli and Palestinian coaches. At Liverpool, after the final whistle has sounded on Chelsea's Champions League campaign, there are congratulations for the victors (*Empics*).

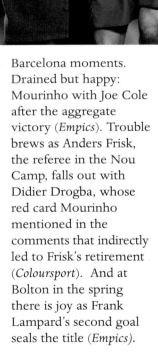

Barcelona moments. Drained but happy: Mourinho with Joe Cole after the aggregate victory (*Empics*). Trouble brews as Anders Frisk, the referee in the Nou Camp, falls out with Didier Drogba, whose red card Mourinho mentioned in the comments that indirectly led to Frisk's retirement (*Coloursport*). And at Bolton in the spring there is joy as Frank Lampard's second goal seals the title (*Empics*).

One of the boys: After Chelsea have clinched the Premiership title at Bolton, John Terry gives Mourinho the sort of hug a player gives to another. In the background are Frank Lampard and Didier Drogba (*Empics*).

Happy family: Mourinho with his wife and children at the UK première of the film *The Incredibles* in London in November 2004. The Mourinhos have followed an old Portuguese custom by passing on their Christian names to their offspring; the son is called José Mario and the daughter Matilde. In order to avoid confusion, they have nicknames (*Getty Images*).

to matters spiritual; he was to remain religious in adulthood, sometimes visiting the shrine at Fátima, a couple of hours' drive to the north of Lisbon.

In 1974, by which time the power of Portuguese football had receded to the extent that Benfica were knocked out of Europe in the early rounds in consecutive seasons – by Derby County and the Hungarian club Újpest Dózsa – José was eleven and something truly significant happened around him. He lived through a revolution. He may not have noticed, because it was a very Portuguese handover of power, a near-bloodless triumph for the forces of democracy, which, to the advantage of José's generation as a whole and José in particular, made educational improvements a high priority. There is a certain irony here. The family benefactor, Mário Ascensao Ledo, had prospered under the old authoritarian regime, the fall of which was followed by a great wave of educational advancement, which José rode. By now Ledo was dead and the canneries had been lost to the revolution – or, as the aunt put it, 'taken by the communists' – but modern Portugal was to serve at least one member of the family well. It is doubtful that José Mourinho would have made a living in football without the key that his academic accomplishments, above all his excellence at languages, were to constitute. For he was never quite good enough at playing to live up to the fond hopes he and his father had entertained. He was no more than what the English used to call a decent amateur.

In 1974, José had still to realise that. He clung to his dreams. Like most adolescents, he cherished his heroes too, and one was Kevin Keegan, who inspired Liverpool's emphatic victory over Newcastle in that year's FA Cup final at Wembley. José supported Liverpool from afar, and when Keegan left for Hamburg in 1977, passed his affections on to Keegan's replacement, Kenny Dalglish; he was also an admirer of Graeme Souness. Those able to cast their minds back to the days when the Scots Dalglish and Souness (with stylish assistance from their compatriot Alan Hansen) were driving Liverpool to supremacy in Europe may have an image of Souness fashioning for Dalglish the goal against Bruges at Wembley that meant the club retained the European title in 1978. It was around that time when reality dawned on Mourinho and he began the process of acceptance that he would never be a top professional footballer. Later, talking it over with his father, he announced that he would instead strive to become the best coach in the world. And Félix, who had himself become a coach after hanging up his goalkeeper's gloves, liked the sound of that, because he already knew his son had a talent for reading the game.

He had encouraged it by giving José tasks to perform for his clubs: early in Félix's coaching career, at Caldas, a little third-division club, he sent José to write assessments of rival teams. As Félix made a growing impact, moving to second-division Amora, near Setúbal, and supervising a successful campaign for promotion to the first division in

1978–79, José also began to learn tricks of the trade: Félix would put him in charge of the ball-boys and have him send messages to players during matches. Coaching came naturally to José and within a few years, having left university, he was looking after Vitória Setúbal's Under-16s.

It was nevertheless important for him to play while he could. Mourinho was a defender. An occasional central midfielder too. But basically a central defender. You may think it odd that, having grown up in the era of Eusébio, an attacker so dynamic and thrilling some judges considered him superior to Pelé, a boy would choose to play at the relatively unglamorous back end of the team. But someone has to defend and José Mourinho, though not physically built in such a way as to suggest he would be a natural bulwark of the rearguard, enjoyed the opportunity that position gave him to organise his colleagues and the game. He is remembered as skilful but not overendowed with speed or the fighting spirit later to be exemplified by his Chelsea captain, John Terry, or the Internazionale team he guided to triumph in the Champions League of 2009–10. Nor was he especially keen on the tireless running coaches crave: a trait later noticeable when, during his widely publicised visit to the Peres Center in Tel Aviv, the Chelsea coach took a somewhat languid part in an informal match. So José Mourinho had a modest playing career, which he combined with school and, after an unscheduled gap year, university studies.

It began in the youth section at Belenenses, where his

father's playing career had finished. Then, when Félix became coach at Rio Ave up in the north, beyond Oporto, he engaged his eighteen-year-old son as a player for one season. Quite a season it was too: Rio Ave finished fifth in the first division, their highest position ever. But José was not able to live at that level. He never got beyond the reserves. He did, however, nearly make it to the first team on the last day of that season. Rio Ave were about to take on Sporting, who needed to win to be sure of the championship, in the Alvalade Stadium in Lisbon when one of their defenders was injured during the warm-up. Félix told his son to get changed. For many years after, José Mourinho disliked being reminded that the club president, José Maria Pinho, countermanded Félix's order. All he said on the matter was vague and general: that because his father was in a difficult position, his appearances were restricted. At Rio Ave there is no record of his having worn the shirt at all. Anyway, it is fair to add that José could hardly have made things much worse that day at the Alvalade: Sporting won 7–0. Father and son returned to their roots and José, upon entering university in Lisbon, played for the reserves at Belenenses, where his father had a second-division season. José went on to have spells with minor clubs in the Setúbal area. And that was about it.

He was a good scholar – all secondary-school pupils in Portugal must learn at least two languages, and Mourinho had no difficulties with that – but not universally brilliant.

In fact poor marks at mathematics disqualified him from entering university at the first attempt. Hence the year up north. He continued his maths studies during that time with his father and repeated the examination before starting at the Instituto Superior de Educaçao Física in Lisbon. There, his gift for languages (he could speak English, French, Spanish and Italian, and several years later, when he went to Barcelona with Bobby Robson, Catalan players and staff were to appreciate his taking the trouble to acquire a grasp of the regional tongue) allowed him to read widely on the physiology and psychology of sporting achievement. He listened intently to the philosophy lectures of Manuel Sérgio, from whom Mourinho began to derive a fascination for playing with people's emotions. The professor remembers him as a voracious student: 'He looked like a cat catching birds.'

After obtaining a degree in sports science, Mourinho taught PE for three years at junior and secondary schools in and around Setúbal – Arangues, Alhos Vedros and Bela Vista – and helped handicapped children to learn sports. One of his former pupils at Arangues, André Chin, recalled Mourinho with warmth: 'He was a very good teacher, very comprehensive in his approach, interested in all the kids. If you had a problem, you could go to him with it. Everybody got along with him. Football was always his big thing. He coached some friends of mine at Vitória Setúbal, youngsters of fourteen or fifteen, and there was one particular kid he thought had potential and tried to help, a black kid called António who went on to play for the Portuguese national youth team. I still see António from time to time. He's a salesman for cable TV. He didn't make it as a player.' This may have been connected with an incident in which António got drunk, overslept, missed training and was hauled out of bed by Mourinho, who told him he could forget joining the rest of the lads on a forthcoming trip to a tournament in France. Or, as André Chin decorously put it: 'I don't think António had quite enough desire or dedication to become a professional footballer.'

It was always like this in the field of youth development: even the most gifted need an inner drive. By now Mourinho's own ambition was focused on coaching. In 1988 he spent a week of his summer break from teaching in Scotland, obtaining the first part of his UEFA coaching licence, and the following season Vitória increased his responsibilities, putting him in charge of their Under-18s as well as the Under-16s. His work impressed the coach, Manuel Fernandes, who was to influence his career greatly. Manuel Fernandes had been an international centre-forward of distinction, with twelve years at Sporting Lisbon before ending his playing career at Vitória and being invited to stay in Setúbal and succeed the veteran English coach Malcolm Allison. In 1990, after two years in charge, Manuel Fernandes joined Estrela da Amadora, a club on the outskirts of Lisbon which had just seized its first major trophy in more than half a century's existence by winning the Portuguese Cup final – and took Mourinho with him.

Mourinho's job as assistant with the title of fitness coach meant he would be working with senior players for the first time. But it was an ill-starred venture. Estrela were relegated at the end of the season and both Manuel Fernandes and Mourinho lost their jobs. At least Mourinho had gained a modicum of European experience at the age of twenty-seven – Estrela overcame the Swiss club Neuchâtel Xamax on penalties before succumbing to FC Liège of Belgium in the second round of the Cup Winners' Cup – but whether that was any consolation as he returned to Setúbal can only be a matter of conjecture. Things were to look up, however, and, when, once again, he took the helping hand of Manuel Fernandes, fate had something much, much better in store. Manuel Fernandes had been in Ovar, a small town in the north that was later to acquire a measure of sporting distinction through the success of its basketball team, and worked for the local club, Ovarense, and it was during this apparently low point of his professional life that he received a call that was to transform a career. Not his – though Fernandes was soon to be back in the top division – so much as Mourinho's.

Mourinho, then, was to be liberally rewarded for the wisdom he had shown in getting those qualifications in Scotland; they were necessary if he was to have any realistic hope of progressing to the heights he envisaged.

But why did he have to go abroad for them? Surprising though it may be, given his own country's contribution to the game, Portugal did not subscribe to the mainstream European coaching curriculum, as used by around forty member countries of UEFA. And why specifically Scotland? 'Coaches came here from all over the world,' recalled Tosh McKinlay, a former Celtic and Scotland player destined to encounter Mourinho much later. 'When I was sixteen or seventeen, they used to ask me to go down – they needed young players as sort of guinea pigs for their training exercises – and I can remember seeing the great Italian coaches like Fabio Capello and Arrigo Sacchi as well as our own, led by Alex Ferguson.' So José Mourinho, having taken advice as to where he should seek his certificate, applied and was accepted for the annual summer course of the Scottish Football Association, held at Largs on the Ayrshire coast.

He arrived with two other Portuguese students and was assigned to a group of fellow foreigners, Americans and Europeans in the main. There were more than 150 students in all. One of the assessors that year was the former Scotland forward Paul Sturrock, later to take charge at St Johnstone, Dundee United, Plymouth Argyle (twice), Southampton, Sheffield Wednesday, Swindon Town and Southend United. 'He didn't stand out,' said Sturrock. 'In fact, I can't remember him.' Sturrock's erstwhile international colleague Gordon Strachan was also there, starting out on the new career that was to take him to

Coventry City, Southampton, Celtic and Middlesbrough. Strachan, too, scratched his head. 'You are put in groups of twelve on these courses,' he said, 'and don't really mix with people from other groups unless you stroll down to the pub for a chat in the evening. Maybe José didn't go to the pub.' Andy Roxburgh remembers the student Mourinho. Just. Roxburgh was Scotland's national coach at the time and he told me: 'I've spoken to José about it since and what he remembers is being impressed that the national team manager of Scotland was also taking the coaching courses.' Yes, but what did Roxburgh himself remember? 'It's very difficult for me to recall every detail of everyone who was on a course.' His assistant Ross Mathie, an SFA stalwart (Roxburgh has for several years been technical director of UEFA), was the course director that year. What's more, he was looking after the international group of aspirants. He said: 'I can definitely picture these three Portuguese guys. In fact, I recall José having a photograph taken with Andy. But I'd be leading you up the garden path if I pretended there was much more I could add.' So, in summary, it might be said that Mourinho's impact on his teachers and fellow students did not lead them to conclude they had been favoured by the presence of greatness.

He had, however, obtained the first half of the requisite certificate at the age of twenty-five and felt the better for it. 'I went back to my young players at Setúbal,' he was later to tell Roxburgh, 'and, because of what I had learned, made a difference.'

Twelve years after that first visit to Largs, he returned – in the extraordinary interim, Mourinho had worked with Bobby Robson and then Louis van Gaal and sat alongside them on the bench while Porto and Barcelona collected trophies galore – to complete his qualification for the UEFA licence. Normally a coach does the two parts of the course in consecutive summers, but Mourinho had been too busy learning at football's university of life, acquiring experience more valuable than any piece of paper as his status (and salary) soared and he worked daily with the likes of Luís Figo, Rivaldo and Ronaldo. He did, however, want that certificate. And, being out of work, he was free to go and get it. So he flew back to Scotland. He could afford business class now.

Among the other students in the European Championship summer of 2000 were Gary Bollan, then a Scottish Premier League player with St Johnstone, who would become a player-coach with Clyde and take charge of Livingston; and Tosh McKinlay, who was playing for Kilmarnock at the time and has since filled a variety of roles from agent to radio analyst. They remember Mourinho. 'As soon as he walked on to that training pitch,' said McKinlay, 'you knew he was different from the rest of us. It was how organised he was, and the way he put things across.'

The students gathered on 24 June, as the European Championship in Holland and Belgium reached the quarter-final stage, and that evening Mourinho watched on television as Portugal beat Turkey 2–0. All four quarter-finals – the other matches ended Italy 2 Romania 0, France 2 Spain 1 and Holland 6 Yugoslavia 1 – were used by Ross Mathie for match-analysis tests. The students sat in the lecture theatre at the Inverclyde Sports Centre with pens and notebooks at the ready and, watching a large screen, logged the matches. Mourinho was on his usual form. He sailed through the exam. As you would expect. 'I was in José's group,' said Gary Bollan, 'and it was immediately obvious that he had come with a coaching background. When he did training exercises, he was much more firm and outspoken than the others. He exuded confidence in his own ability. There was no hesitation, no self-doubt. Of course we'd heard he'd been at Barcelona with Bobby Robson and all that. But José never brought it up, never bragged about it even when we popped down to the pub after finishing for the day. He was a good lad. Very down-to-earth.'

McKinlay agreed: 'It was inspiring to hear him talk about football. We had quite a few chats. One night during the course, they have a dinner and I was sitting next to him. I started by asking him about Jorge Cadete, the Portuguese striker I'd played with at Celtic – José knew him from Sporting Lisbon – and we got on to all sorts of football stuff. Three years later, I bumped into him at Ibrox.' By then Mourinho was in charge of Porto. 'He'd come to Glasgow to watch Celtic play Rangers shortly before they met his team in the UEFA Cup final. I wasn't sure if he'd remember me because he'd become so successful since we last met, but he comes over and says, "Hi – how are you? What are you doing here?" I explained that I was doing a bit of work for Celtic TV. I wished him good luck for the final but added, "You know where my allegiance lies!" He just laughed. Since then I've seen him on the television a lot and I just love listening to the guy because he talks sense.'

Having charmed the Scottish FA's class of 2000, Mourinho flew home with his certificate. At last he was a qualified professional coach. And in the next six years he was to go it alone in spectacular style, winning the national championships of both Portugal and England twice, plus each of the two European titles. Plus four domestic cups. Succeeding, indeed, with such an intensity as to make even a Robson or a Van Gaal gasp. And there was still Inter to come. And Real Madrid.

No wonder much is still said of the benefits of a Scottish education.

Mourinho had, of course, availed himself of quite a bit of supplementary tuition between 1988 and 2000, thanks to his relationship with Manuel Fernandes. Sporting had recalled their erstwhile star forward from Ovar as assistant coach in preparation for the arrival of a big-name foreigner. The trouble was that the new boss, an Englishman, spoke no Portuguese. Manuel Fernandes was talking it over with the president who had invited him back to the club, José Sousa Cintra, when a solution occurred to him: why not engage José Mourinho, who spoke very good English and could act as interpreter? Sousa Cintra readily agreed and, Mourinho having been sent for, the trio went to Lisbon airport to meet the flight from London. Eventually a familiar face came through customs. Mourinho stepped forward. 'Hello, Mister,' he said. For the first time. The first of countless times. Because that is what you call a head coach, regardless of his nationality, in Portugal, and Spain and Italy for that matter. The British taught the world to play football. So, just as the British use the French word for a cook, some nationalities defer to the original masters of the game of football. Sir Bobby Robson, a most patriotic Englishman, never minded that.

'Hello, Mister.
I'm José Mourinho'

Actually what Mourinho said to Bobby Robson upon greeting him that day at Lisbon airport was: 'Hello, Mister. I'm José Mourinho.' And, after handshakes, he went on to explain why he would not be hurrying off; he was to be Robson's interpreter. Robson had had little idea of what he would encounter in a country he had hitherto known only as a very pleasant holiday destination. Of course he knew a fair amount about Portuguese football: he had played against Portugal twice in England's successful qualifying campaign for the 1962 World Cup, and, when England manager, had endured the disappointment of a 1–0 defeat by the Portuguese during the opening phase of the 1986 tournament in Mexico. But he did not know the language. So he was glad to hear this smart young man speak English with such clarity and confidence. Meanwhile an older man, short and tanned and neatly dressed, stood to one side, smiling broadly.

'I am speaking,' Mourinho continued, 'on behalf of the president.' He gestured to the older man, who extended his own hand, and Robson was introduced to Sousa Cintra, his new employer.

On the drive into the city, Robson reflected that it could have been a worse start. 'Two things struck me straight away,' he said. 'The standard of José's English. And the fact that he was a nice-looking boy. Too good-looking for my liking! I remember telling him one day when we were having photographs, "Don't stand next to me, José – you'll make me look ugly."'

Mourinho was supposed to be an interpreter plain and simple. Sousa Cintra's plan was for Manuel Fernandes to be Robson's right-hand man. As soon as Robson had signed his contract in England, the president had announced to the Portuguese media that Manuel Fernandes would return to Sporting as the Englishman's assistant, presumably in order to reassure fans that the club's traditions would be observed. 'Manuel Fernandes could not have done the number-one job,' Robson reflected. 'He wasn't quite a good enough coach at that level. His previous job had been with Ovarense, who have never been in the first division. They are what we'd call a Conference-sized club, I suppose. But he was a very popular figure both within the club and among the fans. José had been working as a schoolteacher and doing a bit of coaching with him. So they'd come to Sporting to be my back-up.'

It was almost inevitable that the language issue would

make Robson lean towards Mourinho: 'He was there with me on the pitch every day. Behind me. While I picked up a little bit of Portuguese.' Hitherto Robson had worked only with English or English-speaking players in his homeland, and Eindhoven, where he went after parting company with the national squad following the World Cup semi-final defeat by Germany on penalties in 1990, was hardly a problem because English is widely spoken in Holland. 'Working with the Portuguese players on the pitch wasn't really a problem for me either – once I'm out there, I've always been able to get by – but every now and again something has to be explained carefully. José was very good. He listened, learned, looked, remembered. He was bright, alert and intelligent. But what I liked best was that, when I'd indicate a player and say to José, "Tell him this, tell him that," I always had the feeling that José was saying it the way I would have said it. That was his knack. He knew he had my backing so he'd tell a player to get closer to his opponent or push up a bit more and they'd respond as if I'd told them. I could see – it was the same reaction. Whether it helped that he came from a footballing background, I don't know, but he had a true bond with me. Also I said to him, "José, I want to know every word these players are saying in the dressing room, what they're saying about the team, and the tactics, and about me. Whatever Figo is muttering about me, you bloody well tell me."'

Those players included Jorge Cadete – later to share

the Celtic dressing room with Tosh McKinlay – as well as Luís Figo, who, though young, was already demonstrating the rich talent that was to make him Portugal's most capped footballer of all time. So Mourinho became Robson's eyes and ears. And mouth, on occasion. 'If I was upset with any player, or needed to get a point over strongly, José wouldn't pull any of my punches. There's always a temptation for an interpreter to do that, but José was very assertive. He never watered down the message. He wasn't afraid. Even with Figo.'

The words Robson used to describe his aide's playing prowess – when, being a man short for an eight against eight or nine against nine in training, he would tell Mourinho to get a bib and take a certain position – were 'keen' and 'enthusiastic'. It was meant kindly. 'He had a certain amount of fitness and, through working with the players, developed it. So, when I used him as a fill-in player, he did all right. When we later went to Barcelona, in fact, he'd be on the same pitch as not only Figo but Ronaldo, Hristo Stoichkov, Pep Guardiola and all the other fantastic players.' Could he move among such company without risking embarrassment? 'Mmm. For a short period. For a twenty-minute practice period. He couldn't do it in a match! But no, he didn't embarrass himself.'

Sporting did. They sacked Robson before his first season was out. Sousa Cintra took a snap decision when Carlos Queiróz (later to become Sir Alex Ferguson's assistant at Manchester United for two spells, before and after a season in charge of Real Madrid, and national coach of Portugal) became available. Manuel Fernandes was shown the door too, as was Mourinho, the pair walking together once more. But Sporting had made a mistake that was to play straight into the hands of their rivals Porto. Shortly afterwards, while Robson was still in Lisbon, he met Mourinho for lunch and declared that Porto had made him an offer. 'José just gasped. "Mister," he said. "Don't let that pass you by. You must go there." And he told me why, explained what a great place it was for football. I asked him if he'd like to come and he said he'd love to.'

At Porto, Robson truly established himself as one of English coaching's most successful exports, emulating his Dutch achievement by winning the national championship twice in a row. And again Mourinho was by his side. On an enhanced salary of £35,000 a year, which was to keep multiplying until, at Barcelona, he became football's highest-paid interpreter. 'I never gave him a coaching job,' said Robson. 'He *assisted*. He expressed my instructions to the players. I never handed the team over to him, even for half an hour, in all the years he was with me. But during our time at Porto he began to offer suggestions. I'd arrive in the morning and say, "José, we're doing this and this, you've seen me work, you know how I want it done," and he might chip in with an idea or two. He was growing into the job.'

Mourinho, in his application to take the Scottish FA course in 2000, stated that he had been 'assistant coach' with Robson at Porto and that was not taking too much of a liberty. 'I did what an assistant coach is meant to do,' he later told an interviewer, 'and with Robson, who lives and breathes for the pitch, that meant planning training sessions.' In fact he did more than that. Robson had noticed that he was an astute reader of the game and decided to send him to spy on forthcoming opponents. 'He'd come back and hand me a dossier that was absolutely first class. I mean first class. As good as anything I've ever received. Here he was, in his early thirties, never been a player, never been a coach to speak of either, giving me reports as good as anything I ever got from the top professional people I'd brought in to scout for me at World Cups when I was with England – Dave Sexton, Howard Wilkinson, the lot. There would be the way the teams played in the match he'd been sent to – both teams – with defence and attack covered very well, patterns of play, nicely set out with diagrams and a different colour for each team. All as clear as a bell. I remember telling him, "Well done, son."

'I think he enjoyed being with me. He loved being on the training pitch and, because I'd come to respect him as a student of the game, I'd sit him down after matches and we'd have long conversations. We'd talk about who'd played well and who hadn't, where we'd gone wrong and what we could do about it.' Several years later, their paths having diverged at Barcelona, Robson was to be in his native north-east of England, reviving Newcastle United, and Mourinho back at Porto, doing much the same thing, this time as the boss, surrounded by his own coterie of assistants. During his first spell at the club, the president, Jorge Nuno Pinto da Costa, had noted his capabilities both on and off the training pitch, said Robson. 'In all my dealings with the president, I'd taken José in with me and he'd fought on my behalf. The president obviously took a shine to him during those meetings. Also he remembered what happened on the pitch in our time. Two championships and a Portuguese Cup in two seasons – you can't do much better than that. And José was by my side all the way. No wonder the president kept an eye on him.'

Porto initially continued to thrive after Robson's departure in 1996 for Barcelona (though a lean spell was to follow, opening the door for Mourinho to return to the club in 2002). Robson had had no hesitation in inviting Mourinho to join him in the new adventure at Barcelona. Indeed the only condition Robson laid down before taking the job was that Mourinho came too. Once again he was to be multi-functional: every time Robson met the Barcelona president, Josep Lluís Núñez, or vice-president, Joan Gaspart, he would be there. The master and his voice were now friends, and when Robson set up home in Sitges, a short drive down the Mediterranean coast from Catalunya's capital, Mourinho did likewise;

he could afford it, too, on a salary that would rise to more than £300,000 a year.

'We saw each other socially,' said Robson. 'My wife, Elsie, became friendly with his wife, Matilde, and we'd all go out for meals together in the evenings. The talk always turned to football. Quite soon after we sat down, usually. What did the wives think? Oh, they understood. They'd just give us a look that said, "Uh-oh, here we go again." Matilde had some interest in the game, a slight knowledge, and sometimes they would listen to us, but she and Elsie were never too intrusive. Basically, they would talk about their things and we would talk about football.'

In the mornings, Robson and Mourinho would drive into the city, to a training ground lying in the shadow of the Camp Nou, a massive stadium holding more than 100,000 spectators, to exercise Barcelona's thoroughbred players. At first it was a trial for Mourinho, who, unlike Robson, had no standing in the game. 'They didn't know who he was – and made that quite plain. Also they questioned whether, not having been a player of any standard himself, he was entitled to be telling them what to do. But he won them over.' Gradually, the key figures in the dressing room came to accept he had a lot to offer: skilfully edited videos, for instance, illustrating strengths or weaknesses of opponents, were especially appreciated by the more thoughtful players. Pep Guardiola, an elegant force on the field, a ringmaster or *pivote* stationed in front of the defence, who had emerged from the youth academy and become a key figure in the 'Dream Team' under Johan Cruyff that had brought the club its first European title in 1992, was a Catalan, which served to embed him in the supporters' hearts. 'He was a big fish,' said Robson. 'A good player too. He had his opinions on the game, Guardiola, and I didn't mind that. He'd say we couldn't play this way or we couldn't do that – he had an opinion on everything. José saw that he was an important figure within the club and said to himself, "I've got to get to know him, I've got to get in with this guy." And he did. José and Pep were quite friendly. They respected each other. And, of course, José could speak to Pep.' In Spanish or, eventually, Catalan.

In time, Guardiola and Mourinho were to become reacquainted through one of the game's great rivalries: that between Barcelona and Real Madrid. Guardiola, having been placed in charge at Barcelona in 2008, guided the club to the Champions League title in his first season. Mourinho, after leading Inter to that honour the following season, joined Real. Robson did not live to see Guardiola's Barcelona triumph 5–0 over Mourinho's Real in the first Clasico of 2010–11; cancer had finally claimed the much-loved Englishman in 2009.

He had been happy to reminisce about Mourinho and the formative times with the stars who trained by Camp Nou. 'José gradually built up a rapport with the squad,' Robson said. 'The players liked him. He even joined in a bit of banter with them. He got close to Ronaldo, which helped.' The young Brazilian was to become the biggest name in the game – world and European player of the year – after Barcelona took Robson's insistent advice to buy him from PSV Eindhoven, a former club of Robson's. 'Ronaldo took to José quite quickly. José was in a good position with the players generally because he didn't pick the side – I did. So, if a player was left out, he blamed me, not José. I had to keep a distance from the players, as a manager does. José could cross over that line and come back again.' He did too. As at Sporting Lisbon and Porto, he would spy on not only the opposition's players but, at Robson's behest, his own team's. Take the case of Hristo Stoichkov. 'A strange one,' said Robson. 'I'd been worried about Stoichkov.' The greatest Bulgarian footballer ever, Stoichkov had a reputation for living up to his dark and brooding appearance. 'I'd heard he was a difficult character to have around the club. Yet I found him quite the opposite. He was a pro who didn't muck about in training – he trained right and played right. I'd thought he'd be a surly, unsmiling, unsociable Iron Curtain type. He wasn't. And José got very friendly with him. So did I in the end. But José knew him better because José would mix with the players. He and Stoichkov were very friendly. They used to talk about the team a lot. And José would pass it on to me. But I liked Stoichkov and I trusted him.'

Just as Mourinho had overshadowed Manuel Fernandes

at Sporting Lisbon, he was closer to Robson than the ostensible number two at Barcelona, José Ramón Alexanco, a former club captain. In Robson's one season in charge of the team, 1996–97, Barcelona won the European Cup Winners' Cup, beating Paris St Germain in the final through a Ronaldo penalty, and the Spanish Cup, but finished two points behind their arch-rivals Real Madrid in the championship. Robson nevertheless assumed this would be enough to persuade Núñez and the other directors to let him fulfil the second year of his contract. He was wrong. While the financial terms of the contract would be honoured, he was to give way to Louis van Gaal, the Dutch coach who had guided Ajax to the European title two years earlier. Robson was to become 'general manager' and take other duties, such as travelling the world in search of suitable talent. Suddenly Barcelona had in Mourinho and Robson not only the most lavishly remunerated of interpreters but, as Robson himself ruefully put it, 'the world's highest-paid scout'.

He went to a meeting – accompanied by Mourinho, naturally – with Núñez, Gaspart and Van Gaal and expressed his disappointment. But Van Gaal was assured by Robson that, if the president saw him as Barcelona's future, there would be no further dispute between them, and Van Gaal said he appreciated that. Robson, already in his mid-sixties, was to have further coaching posts at PSV in Eindhoven, again, and Newcastle United. What, though, was to become of Mourinho? His first instinct, said Robson, was to quit, head home to Portugal – 'José didn't like what had happened to me' – and ponder his future. But Robson went to Van Gaal and advised the Dutchman to keep Mourinho. 'I told him, "Louis, he knows the city, he knows the club, he knows the players. He speaks fantastic Spanish and can do for you what he's done for me. He's an asset." So he stayed with Louis. And he got to do a little more work. A bit of coaching. That's because Louis is different from me. I have to be in full control, hands-on. Louis is one of those guys – the Sven-Göran Eriksson type – who like to stand back. Louis would even hand over the team to José for friendlies. That was great experience for him.'

In the summer of 1998, Robson went to Eindhoven, where there was no job for Mourinho (it was a short-term assignment). Robson rang to tell him so and advised Mourinho to keep learning under Van Gaal. Until the following September, when Newcastle sacked Ruud Gullit and brought Robson out of retirement. Again he rang Mourinho. 'I said, "There could be a job for you here at Newcastle, but I'll have to get my feet under the table first. In the meantime, work out what you want to do."' By the time Robson was ready to make him an offer, almost exactly a year later, Mourinho was on home soil, waiting for a suitable club and ready to be judged as a coach in his own right. 'He asked me what I thought of the idea. "Give it a go," I said.' He did. He got the Benfica job. And lasted just three turbulent months.

'When I heard he'd gone from Benfica,' said Robson, 'I thought maybe the job had been too much for him, that he wasn't quite there yet. But there were reasons for his leaving which explained it.' Club politics, essentially.

I asked Robson what he had had in mind for Mourinho at Newcastle and he replied: 'I just saw him as an important member of the staff. I saw him scouting, doing match appraisals, looking at players. But I also envisaged using him on the training pitch every day, giving him more responsibility on the coaching side and letting that develop.' No doubt many Newcastle supporters have fantasised about what might have happened to their club had Robson groomed Mourinho as his successor, prepared him to command a stripe-shirted institution as passionately supported as Porto but with, at that time, more of the resources required to finance a Champions League campaign such as that which culminated gloriously for the Portuguese club in 2004.

According to Mourinho, that is what Robson laid on the table, a vague notion of the succession, without even tempting him to take it seriously; Mourinho simply could not believe that Robson would ever stand back from the team until he retired from football completely, and told him so. Robson also recalled a less than clear-cut proposal: 'Obviously it was understood that he'd be maturing all the time and I'd not be getting any younger. But I'm not sure that I saw that level of capability in him at that stage. I mean it. It wasn't a question of doubting him. I knew he was bright. I knew he could handle players. I didn't know he had enough technical knowledge to be his own man.' Surely the thought had occurred, however fleetingly, when Mourinho handed in those spot-on scouting reports, that here was a tip for the top? 'One thing doesn't necessarily follow the other. And, as far as being a principal coach is concerned, I didn't know he had any ambition in that direction.' Amazing. Such reticence from the young man we were to see, just a few short years later, relentlessly destroying all the giants of the profession strewn in his path – and boasting about it. 'He had humility then,' said Robson. 'Throughout the time we were together, he showed me respect. He knew what my position was and where he stood. He never tried to rise above his station.'

There was a story that, when they were at Barcelona, players who understood English formed an impression that Mourinho was not simply translating Robson's instructions but amplifying them slightly. Did Robson ever suspect that? He grinned. 'Well, I wouldn't know, would I? No, I never had the feeling that the message was anything other than precisely as I'd intended. José did a great job and he was very loyal to me.' Nor did Robson notice the cockiness, the contentiousness towards opponents or the propensity for getting up people's noses. Not much anyway; there was a tunnel fracas after a match against Athletic Bilbao when the Basque club's coach, Luis Fernández, was said to have pointed a disapproving finger at him. But the Mourinho who was to be presented to the sports fans of Portugal and with whom we, the English audience, were to grow familiar – the unpredictable, sometimes exasperating and almost always enthralling Mourinho – had yet to rise to the surface of his personality. As Robson said: he had humility then.

A little bit of arrogance

Louis van Gaal did not blame Mourinho for getting upset with Barcelona over their treatment of Bobby Robson. The Dutchman was speaking to me in Sitges, in the apartment he retained there; the Van Gaals, like the Robsons, were neighbours of the Mourinhos. 'It was a strange situation when I arrived,' said Van Gaal. 'I had initially been engaged as director of youth development. Then suddenly the president changed his mind and wanted me to be coach with Robson in charge of scouting. Now Robson had won three trophies in the season just finished. But, being a gentleman, he didn't show his anger. Mourinho showed anger! His position would be disappearing as well, of course, because as coach I would be bringing my assistants from Holland with me. But when we had this meeting with Núñez and Gaspart I was encountering Mourinho for the first time – and I was impressed with his personality. I knew I needed help with Spanish, having had only one week at a language school in the Netherlands, so I told the president it would be convenient if Mourinho, who also knew the players, would stay as my assistant, my third assistant [behind Gerard van der Lem and Frans Hoek, who had worked with Van Gaal at Ajax]. So he was kept on, initially for a year. To start with he was just a translator, but gradually he became as valued as my other assistants. He could read the game and he analysed the opposition so well that, after my first year, when we won the Spanish championship and Cup, I was happy for him to stay for three years.'

In the second of those years, Mourinho worked with the first team. 'I like to give responsibility to my assistants,' said Van Gaal. 'I like them to take all or part of a training session because, if the head coach trains the players all the time, in the end they stop listening to you. A coach has to observe and correct, but there is only so much correcting you can do before, psychologically, they switch off. So sometimes I like to stand back. But in order to do that you have to be confident in the quality of your assistants. In José's case, I started with him by my side. Then, as is normal, we divided the players into three groups – Frans Hoek with the goalkeepers and the others split between Gerard van der Lem and José – and once I had seen how José handled it I knew I could trust him. I am a believer in ball possession and positional play. So we do a lot of positional play in a session. Then you can see if someone can really coach. And he could. He could see what the players had to do. Also there was the quality of his analyses. The players saw them and, if players get the feeling that the coach can read the game better than they themselves can, they listen. I decided he was good enough to take charge of the team in friendly matches. He did a lot of those, plus games in the Catalan Cup, which could be not so friendly because Barcelona's local rivals, Espanyol, and the lower-division clubs took them seriously, as did the media.' Van Gaal was always present, lest any of his players be tempted to doubt Mourinho's authority. 'This was my only reservation,' said Van Gaal. 'I'd seen enough to know he could really coach. I'd seen him give the talks to the players at half-time. If I had felt the need to intervene, I would have done. I just didn't know if he could do it when I wasn't there. To get to the very top, you must be able not only to organise players but handle a team, to find that chemistry. That's the difference.'

Van Gaal, like Robson, never noticed in Mourinho a burning ambition. 'I never even noticed a restlessness. But then we were a team. We spoke about what he did – not what he wanted. Maybe he spoke about it to other people.'

Although Van Gaal has a reputation for being stern and dour, he and his wife, Truus, enjoy their time off and they would get together with the Mourinhos for meals or children's birthday parties. 'I know the journalists think I don't like to socialise,' said Van Gaal, 'but I do.

José and Matilde, who became close friends with Truus, had an apartment in the same park as ours, so, if he was late in completing his analysis of our next opponents, he'd just bring it round and stay for a chat. I liked him. He was a little bit arrogant, not always a respecter of reputations, but I like that. I like people with a high opinion of themselves and like to surround myself with them. I don't want yes-men, because you need people who will say, "No – there is another way." He could do that. And he did. I encouraged it. I told him to include in his analyses how *he* would play against this opposition. I have always stimulated that sort of contribution but, because of José's special qualities as an analyst, I paid a little more attention to him than my other assistants in this respect. And, OK, it's always the head coach who decides how the team will play – but I certainly wanted to hear José's point of view.'

The truth, by Mourinho's own account, is that he had become restless at Barcelona, impatient for the power to direct operations, beset by a curiosity to discover if he could follow in Van Gaal's footsteps and be his own man. Van Gaal regards the football the team played in his third year with Mourinho as the best of his time in charge, even though they failed to complete a hat-trick of Spanish championships and lost to Valencia in the semi-finals of the Champions League. 'It was just that we had a lot of trouble with Rivaldo, who had been voted world player of the year and decided in the middle of the season that he didn't want to play on the left side any more. Because he refused to play where he was asked to play – because, in effect, he withdrew his labour – I left him out of the team, and the disruption it caused meant we didn't quite fulfil our potential. There was a lot of criticism of the president and he quit. Out of loyalty, I quit also. The assistants had to go too. Especially Mourinho.' When I expressed surprise, Van Gaal chuckled. 'I sometimes think I was the only guy who believed in José. Because, when Robson left and I insisted José had to stay, they weren't pleased. He was known as *El Traductor* [The Translator]. The media called him that. When I first came to the club, even the president called him that, but I always spoke about José as a football man and gradually all the officials started to treat him with the respect due to one of my assistants. I took him more seriously than most people in the club, I think – because I was in a position to judge him.'

Benfica's loss is Porto's gain

When Mourinho returned to Portugal in June 2000, it was to a state of unemployment. Very much self-imposed, to judge from his version, which was that he had no wish to stay at Barcelona, being unimpressed by their choice of Llorenç Serra Ferrer as Van Gaal's successor. Mourinho did not believe that the Majorcan, who had been working with the club's youths, had much chance of success at the higher level (Ferrer was to be dismissed after eleven months) and was reluctant to work under him. Van Gaal doubted that the new man would have wanted Mourinho around anyway: 'I'd installed Serra Ferrer as head of youth education and I don't recall he and Mourinho had a good relationship.' What's more, Mourinho had grown tired of the subordinate's life. In the last of his three years at Barcelona, he had become increasingly frustrated and had often come home to his wife in a grumpy mood as he analysed Van Gaal's decisions and compared them unfavourably with those he would have taken. His mind was made up: he had to be number one, even if it meant taking a big drop in pay.

He had a reputation in Portugal. While in Barcelona, he had received the odd offer from his homeland, the most attractive from Sporting Braga the previous year, and he imagined some such middle-range club would suit him best. Mourinho was in no hurry – he had built up a respectable bank account while in Barcelona – and spent the rest of the summer either at his home in Setúbal or in the Algarve, where he had bought a holiday place near Portimao. There were football books and videos to study and there was time to start collating his thoughts on coaching in a computer document for strictly private use, which, presumably without a hint of irony or embarrassment, admirers have come to call his 'bible'. There was a family to enjoy – his daughter was four and his son a baby – and the sun shone.

September came and Mourinho, having spurned Robson's offer to come to Newcastle, was in Setúbal when the phone rang. On the line was Eládio Paramés, a former football journalist who had become director of communications at Benfica. He told Mourinho that the club's president, Joao Vale e Azevedo, had a proposition to put. Mourinho, aware that Benfica already had a coach, Jupp Heynckes, said he was no longer interested in being anyone's assistant, but Paramés persuaded him to see the president, who confirmed that the job on offer was the German incumbent's.

Although you could hardly call Benfica a humble beginning for Mourinho's career as a coach, the club had fallen a long way from the heights occupied in the years of his infancy: the Eusébio years, when they could look any European club in the eye. They were skint and struggling and could barely keep pace with the likes of Sporting Braga, let alone their great rivals Sporting and Porto. But there was still the Benfica name, with all it entailed in terms of tradition and size of support; Mourinho had to give the president a hearing.

Vale e Azevedo told him the club indeed had no money, so he wanted Mourinho to build a team with hungry, young, Portuguese – or, to put it another way, cheap – players. Oh, and the contract would be for only six months because there was an election for the club presidency coming up (the leaders of most clubs in Portugal were chosen by the members) and that would take place in a matter of six weeks or so. That was the bad news. The good news was that Vale e Azevedo was expected to win and, as and when that happened, Mourinho would be given a two-year extension. Mourinho took the chance, took the job. Vale e Azevedo lost the election.

The winner, Manuel Vilarinho, had run on a ticket that proclaimed Benfica's next coach would be Toni, a former star player, and Vilarinho's first statement was that he hoped Mourinho, being a man of honour, would recognise his duty to step aside, so it could be said that their relationship was getting off to a tricky start. But Mourinho, after receiving an assurance from Vilarinho that he could continue until at least the end of the season, got on with the job. He made the players train less casually and railed at the backroom staff for providing dodgy dossiers – one report listed only ten men in the opposition's team – and generally strove to change the club's culture. Then, in his ninth match, they achieved a remarkable 3–0 home victory over Sporting. Few victories are sweeter than in a derby, yet the taste can turn bitter when a coach is consumed by righteous indignation and, as Vilarinho appeared at the door of Mourinho's office while he was speaking on the phone to his wife, the president was ignored. Furthermore, Mourinho declined to speak to the press, assured Benfica staff he would pay the ensuing fine and drove home.

Next he attempted to force Vilarinho's hand. He asked for a year's extension to his contract, on the pretext that another club had expressed interest in him – and the reply could be most charitably described as lukewarm. Yes, said Vilarinho, I'd happily keep you on; it's just that some of the other directors, and our commercial partners, are not sure. It was agreed that Mourinho would leave immediately. His team's derby triumph had a more orthodox consequence when Sporting's coach, Augusto Inácio, was sacked. And guess who moved into that job? Manuel Fernandes, Mourinho's old friend and partner, the man who had recommended he be hired as Bobby Robson's interpreter. Toni, of course, got the Benfica job. So Mourinho's first solo flight was all too quickly over. It had lasted barely a couple of months. But, as Robson later said, the circumstances had made that almost inevitable.

It was nearly Christmas. Almost exactly four years before Mourinho and his wife were to take the children ice-skating near Sloane Square in London.

Mourinho waited at home in Setúbal until mid-April, when he took a call from a representative of the Uniao club of Leiria in the Portuguese midlands and agreed to take over from Manuel José at the end of the season. Leiria were already doing well and finished fifth that season, their highest position ever, but Mourinho had them in fourth place as, once again, Christmas approached and things started happening. Benfica sacked Toni and offered Mourinho his job back – he declined after it became clear there was no room at the club for Baltemar Brito and Rui Faria, who had become the first members of a team of assistants destined to share in his fame – and then Porto beckoned. The president, Jorge Nuno Pinto da Costa, had assured him at an international match in Oporto several months earlier that he would take command when the time was right. Just after Christmas, an intermediary's call informed him the time had almost arrived and in January he replaced Octávio Machado.

Porto, like Benfica, had a proud history. They, too, had been champions of Europe. Just once, but more recently than Benfica – in 1987. The current Porto team, said Mourinho, was their worst for twenty-six years – he would have remembered the mid-1970s, for in those days Porto frequently trailed in behind Vitória Setúbal, whose Bonfim Stadium was his second home and for whom his father kept goal – but no matter, Mourinho added: 'Next year we'll win the League.' They did.

For the first time since he had attained headline-commanding status, Mourinho had done what it said on the tin. He had begun to rebuild in the remaining months of his first season, setting up deals to bring in the likes of Maniche, Nuno Valente, Paulo Ferreira, all of whom went on to represent Portugal, and Derlei, whom Mourinho had found in Brazil while preparing for his time at Leiria and brought to that club at a knockdown price. Cast aside, sometimes quite unceremoniously, were those he perceived to be of faint heart or unsuitable head. The broad strategy was to make the team more Portuguese in character and hungrier (through incentive-based contracts) and early in the new season he made a tactical switch to the 4–4–2 formation with which European glory was to be seized. He had fashioned a disciplined, resilient unit.

But Mourinho's Porto were already more than that. In Deco, also born in Brazil but to be claimed by Portugal, for whom he was to take part in the 2004 European Championship, they had an artful playmaker and he was prominent as Porto proved they also had the sophistication to operate successfully outside Portugal's borders by winning the UEFA Cup after a long and, on occasion, turbulent campaign, the bargain buy Derlei finally putting paid to Celtic with his eleventh goal in the competition. While Porto's players celebrated in front of their fans, very much a minority in Seville's Olympic Stadium, some 40,000 supporters of the Scottish champions indicated by scornful gesture that Mourinho's men were a bunch of divers (in truth, though Deco and company were not unacquainted with the art of obtaining free-kicks, the frequency with which they fell had as much to do with Celtic's rough approach). Mourinho had supervised a remarkable, and merited, triumph.

He did get one thing wrong. Asked how his team would cope with the even greater rigours of the Champions League the following season, he replied: 'We can do some nice things ... but I don't think we can win it.' He explained that such aspirations were only for the 'sharks', whom he defined as 'clubs who can afford to spend 20, 30 or even 40 million euros on one player'. Porto hardly caused a ripple in the market that summer. Yet, with virtually the same team, they went on to win the Champions League.

So had Mourinho's modest assessment been a psychological ploy, designed to take the pressure of expectation off his players? Not this time. I think that, for once, he genuinely surprised himself and only developed a conviction they could defeat the odds after the dramatic survival of a second-round visit to Manchester United, where, a linesman's verdict on Paul Scholes having crucially gone their way, Costinha scored a stoppage-time winner and Mourinho wildly celebrated on the touchline.

A less judicious man might have missed it all by leaving after the UEFA Cup triumph. He did briefly consider the possibility of cashing in. Inevitably, there were offers from abroad that would have doubled or tripled his salary: from Paris St Germain and a couple of mid-range Italian clubs. Among those confidants he consulted was Robson. 'I told him to stay another year,' said the Englishman, whose Newcastle had just finished third in the Premier League, a position that meant they could themselves qualify for the Champions League if they beat Partizan Belgrade over two legs, which they were clear favourites to do. 'I told José, "You've got time on your side. Don't get into a cage unless you know how to get out of it. You're not ready to move yet. I was at Ipswich fourteen years – you've been at Porto barely fourteen months! So stay for at least a year. Apart from anything else, the president has taken a chance with you. Yes, you've done well for him. You've had a wonderful year. But you might learn more next year if you stay and get more experience."' It proved good advice. Meanwhile Robson was unable to join Mourinho in the Champions League. Newcastle, after winning 1–0 in Belgrade, succumbed by an identical score at home and lost the penalty decider. Oddly enough, the subsequent draw for the group stages put Partizan in with Porto; fate was that close to laying on a contest between the erstwhile master and his pupil. It was never to happen, for, after Mourinho came to England, his first encounter with Newcastle took place three months after Robson had been sacked.

As it was, Porto had to deal with Real Madrid as well as Partizan and Olympique Marseille. If the big and financially muscular clubs of Europe could be likened by Mourinho to sharks, Real were the Great Whites of the European game; they did not even recognise his 40 million euro limit, having spent considerably more than that on the world's most expensive player, Zinedine Zidane. Other *galácticos* who came to test Porto included Roberto Carlos, Mourinho's old Barcelona chum Ronaldo and an even more familiar face: Luís Figo. Real won 3–1. It looked as if Mourinho's analysis of the relationship between money and Champions League success was right; Porto had been severely bitten. But they healed their wounds by beating Marseille twice (the French club were later to remove poor Robson's Newcastle from the UEFA Cup) and qualified for the knockout stages in second place.

Although they came from behind to beat Manchester United with two goals from Benni McCarthy in the new Dragao Stadium, they were not expected to preserve the lead in the face of a shark attack at Old Trafford and duly Scholes put United in front midway through the first half. Later Scholes scored again, or would have done had the linesman not erred in ruling him offside. 'Porto would never have come back from 2–0,' said Robson, 'and that was the only major slice of luck they got in the competition.' Given that United led on the away-goals rule, it would still not have been enough but for Costinha's swift reaction to a rebound off the United goalkeeper, Tim Howard, as the majority of a 67,000 crowd prepared to celebrate the final whistle. As Mourinho put it: 'My team were out after ninety minutes – and in the quarter-finals after ninety-one.'

Lyon were next and the decisive manner in which the French were overcome sharpened appetites for the semi-final against Deportivo La Coruña. The first leg, at Porto, was dull and goalless, but Mourinho and his team did not appear too despondent and a fortnight later, on a stormy night by the Bay of Biscay, we discovered why: they clearly believed they could win at the Riazor, even though Milan, the reigning champions, had been thrashed there in the previous round. With Costinha shackling the creative abilities of Deportivo's elegant Juan Carlos Valerón, the opportunity was there for an away goal to settle matters. Deco – slippery as an eel, persistent as a terrier – did the trick after an hour, tempting the stand-in defender César to try a tackle the Spaniard was not sharp enough to execute legitimately and falling just inside the penalty area. Derlei did the rest. Porto were in the final.

It was to be against little Monaco, who had not only removed Real Madrid but were to overcome a Chelsea backed by the billions of Roman Abramovich. So much for Europe's sharks. It was the year of the minnows. Well, the smaller fish. You know what I mean. Mourinho, like the rest of us, had underestimated the power of football to overcome economics. It must have been the only thing he had neglected to learn during his prolonged and comprehensive education.

By now he was established above Didier Deschamps, the Monaco coach, as Chelsea's choice for the next season and this, despite the Italian alternative presented by Inter, was an offer he could hardly refuse. Peter Kenyon, having been unable to get Sven-Göran Eriksson to Chelsea, was falling on his feet. After the match in La Coruña, Mourinho, brow furrowing as he fiddled with his mobile phone – 'at moments like these, you want to speak to your loved ones' – declined to discuss his future, but the next morning he flew from Oporto to London with his wife and children and in the evening, accompanied by a posse of Portuguese journalists, he went to Stamford Bridge, where Monaco's second-leg victory in the other semi-final ensured that the Champions League would not be culminating in a contest between his present and future employers; it must have been quite a relief, even to such an expert exuder of indifference as Mourinho.

Next there was some domestic business to attend to. The retention of the Portuguese championship had already been achieved but the task of keeping the Cup in Porto loomed, with a final against Benfica due ten days before the European climax in Gelsenkirchen. Mourinho, aware that Monaco's Deschamps would be watching, altered and slightly weakened his team, who were reduced to ten men in the second half when Jorge Costa was sent off. They nevertheless played well enough to be level at a goal each after ninety minutes, but Simão scored for Benfica in extra time and afterwards Mourinho decried the referee's performance. He was quoted as having called the official – Lucílio Batista, from Mourinho's own home city of Setúbal – a cheat, but Batista's report referred only to constant querying of decisions from the Porto bench. It was not a first offence. Mourinho was ordered to pay a fine of 600 euros, which the records of the Portuguese Football Federation show him to have duly done, and to serve a suspension of fifteen days, which he avoided by leaving Portugal for England. Via Germany.

The event in Gelsenkirchen was affected, as Mourinho generously volunteered afterwards, by an early injury that deprived Monaco of their captain, Ludovic Giuly. 'It changed the face of the match,' Mourinho said, 'and enabled us to play the football we like to play.' Which was on the counter-attack. Carlos Alberto got the first of three unanswered goals in the first half and, after Dmitri Alenitchev had replaced the Brazilian youngster on the hour, Deco, with a piece of deliciously impudent finishing, and the substitute put Monaco out of their discomfort. The scenes at the end were of the usual delirium, except that Mourinho had a subdued look and stayed close to his wife and children. He also chose not to exhibit his medal, removing the ribbon from his neck after the presentation, and later told Andy Roxburgh: 'On a personal level, the night was difficult because I was full of conflicting emotions, knowing that I would be leaving the team – I did not see my Porto players again until three months later when they came to Stamford Bridge in the Champions League.' Apart from Paulo Ferreira and Ricardo Carvalho, that was; he wasted no time in bringing them to Chelsea and tried to lure Deco, who chose Barcelona instead. Mourinho had become a shark.

Before embarking on his predatory activities, he revisited London to brief Chelsea staff and agents and meet the media, who, upon asking why he was so confident about the prospects for a club who had last won their domestic championship eight years before he was born, responded: 'We have top players and – excuse me if I'm arrogant – a top manager ... please don't call me arrogant, because it's not true. I think I'm a special one. I'm a champion.' Having also dealt with more esoteric matters, such as the balance of responsibilities within his coaching department (we did not trouble our newspapers' readers with that), and outlined his disciplinary code (we printed it, albeit without reference to its uncanny similarity to that of other coaches), he flew to Brazil for a ten-day family holiday. The midsummer he spent commenting for a Portuguese newspaper on the European Championship, which was being held in his homeland. How strange to reflect that he had watched some of the previous European Championship in Scotland while completing his coaching qualifications; now he was the most fêted coach in the world! Then he took his new charges off to the United States to prepare for a season that, being Mourinho-influenced, was bound to be momentous.

Until that late May evening on which Mourinho's previous season reached its glorious conclusion, the abiding image had been of his touchline dance in his overcoat at Old Trafford. In my mind this was superseded by the tutorial Mourinho gave Alenitchev in the technical area shortly before he ran on to the field to take over from Carlos Alberto. It lasted several minutes and involved much pointing at a notepad. Usually a substitute gets little more than a quick word and a pat on the bottom; Mourinho's attention to detail was fascinating (and his method of getting the point over was to become fashionable). Fifteen minutes and two goals later, the job was done. The following spring, while Mourinho was carrying all in England and Europe before him, a seasoned observer of the game told me he was overrated. 'What he does,' my friend opined, 'is painting by numbers.' Such respect does my friend command that I lacked the heart to reply that, if that were the case, we should all be doing it, and picking up several million pounds a year for our trouble.

PART FOUR

José who?

The three hats

Andy Roxburgh, the former Scotland manager whose job it became to monitor the work of the coaching profession's most distinguished exponents, described José Mourinho as the product of an advantageous upbringing and an ideal education, supplemented by 'the finest example of work experience in the history of employment'.

Apart from that, he never had much going for him.

When Roxburgh visited Mourinho at Chelsea in 2005, Mourinho made a wry quip: 'After fifteen years, I'm an overnight success.' The UEFA technical director understood. It is less important for a coach setting out on his career to be instantly recognisable to millions than to have learned the elements of his craft. The fame and fortune that go with being a star footballer can mask an inability to cope with the retraining process. Mourinho was once asked why so many players who had failed to reach a high level, either through injury or for other reasons, went on to succeed as coaches. His reply was swift and simple: 'More time to study.' While the game's chosen ones are still playing, the rejects are learning and, increasingly, they are landing the top jobs.

In this respect, then, Mourinho is nothing special. Among those who have coached teams to Champions League or UEFA Cup honours after playing careers ranging from the unsung to the barely existent are Arrigo Sacchi, Ottmar Hitzfeld, Rafael Benítez and Gérard Houllier. Marcello Lippi, Louis van Gaal and Sir Alex Ferguson, though respected professionals in Italy, Holland and Scotland respectively, were never called to represent their countries. Brazil's triumph in the World Cup of 2002 was overseen by a non-international: Luiz Felipe Scolari. So was Greece's in the European Championship of 2004: by Otto Rehhagel. And Italy's coach in the 2006 World Cup was Lippi. Few leading football nations have former star players in charge of their squads. By and large, those who employ coaches are coming to understand that it is a specialist job for which the ability to send a crowd into paroxysms of delight with a swivel of your hips is not necessarily the prime qualification.

When Roxburgh became Scotland's coach, he was greeted by 'Andy Who?' headlines. Which, given that his entire playing career had taken place in Scotland, right under the headline-writers' noses, must have been slightly hurtful. But he was in good company. The

English newspapers had much the same reaction to Arsène Wenger's appointment at Arsenal. 'There is still a public perception,' said Roxburgh, 'that in order to be a competent coach you have to have been a famous player. But it's not always the case. There are many examples of very famous players – wonderful, instinctive players – who were absolutely useless as coaches or managers. Then you have the reverse – people like Arrigo Sacchi. He wasn't even a professional player.' Yet he built, at Milan, one of the best club sides in the history of the European game. And then guided Italy to the World Cup final in 1994. When they lost on penalties to a Brazil team supervised by Carlos Alberto Parreira, who had never kicked a ball professionally either. 'Now I'm not denying that to have been a top player is an advantage,' Roxburgh continued, 'if the other attributes are in place.' As in the cases of, say, Johan Cruyff, or Fabio Capello, a distinguished player with Juventus and Italy who, having succeeded Sacchi at Milan, immediately established himself as an outstanding coach. 'The top player starts with the experience and the players immediately respect him and listen to him. But it is only a start. Guys like José and, before him, Arrigo Sacchi have had to earn that respect. They've had to work even harder than the former star player.'

Houllier loves to quote Sacchi on this topic. Asked how he could coach without having played, the Italian replied: 'I didn't realise you had to have been a horse to be a jockey.' The functions were completely different, said Houllier: 'When you are a player, you focus on your career. When you are a coach, you focus on everything. Stuart Pearce was eloquent about it. He said that, when he became a player-manager at Nottingham Forest, it hit him like a revelation.' It did not put him off permanently, for Pearce, having obtained his qualifications and worked under Kevin Keegan at Manchester City, took responsibility for that club's fortunes and later ended up in charge of the England Under-21s, being groomed as a possible successor to Fabio Capello. Maybe he will make the transition. Houllier's own playing habitat was the French third division and subconsciously, he said, he might have been driven to compensate for unfulfilled dreams by developing the instinct to organise others. Like Mourinho, he was lucky to have paternal guidance. 'My father was in charge of a local team near Boulogne and showed me how to do things. When I was a player, I started going to analyse the opposition, just for fun mainly, though the coach did find it helpful. José has spoken highly of his father and what he gained through being the son of a coach.'

Even as he approached the end of his time at university, Mourinho would do the occasional spying stint for his father. Félix, his coaching career having peaked in two spells at Rio Ave – the latter featured an appearance in the Portuguese Cup final, which Porto won 4–1 – began moving from one lower division club to another, usually involuntarily. Still José stayed close to him. But the young Mourinho had to think about earning a living and even then he took a direction that served his future interests well, as Roxburgh explained: 'He had trained to be a teacher.' Again Roxburgh, as a former teacher, might be biased, but he insisted there were countless examples of how a teaching background could help to prepare a coach: to name only a couple of the more prominent Dutch ones, Van Gaal and the late, revered Rinus Michels. 'Rinus would always say his teaching background had been invaluable. After all, teaching is about communication and organisation – and so is coaching. Then, having established that building block in his career, José went to find the next, educating himself in coaching by going on courses like the one he did with us in Scotland. This gave him the global method of training, which he still uses.' It involves the development of technical, tactical and fitness elements together, through the medium of compressed small-sided games, and, said Roxburgh, had been formulated by the SFA to suit the mentality of Scots, who 'get easily bored and don't like drills and things like that'.

More than a decade later, when Mourinho took charge at Leiria, he surveyed the location for pre-season training with the president, who gazed at the nearby hills and valleys and observed that they would be ideal for running. Mourinho told him to forget the scenery; the players would be running only on the pitch. Did that resonate with Roxburgh? 'Absolutely. Our mentality was all to do with the pitch. It was portable goals and small-sided games, double-penalty-box games, wingers' games – an endless stream of games. The players would be learning without realising it. José has, of course, had many influences along the way. But he still has this global view. At Chelsea his fitness trainer, Rui Faria, would rarely work detached from the coaching itself. He would stand beside José and advise him on decisions about when to extend the pitch or widen it, or highlight a certain aspect, or increase the intensity of an exercise, change the speed, make it two-touch or whatever. Everything was done together.'

Robson introduced him to a different approach. 'With Bobby,' said Roxburgh, 'he could begin to learn like a fly on the wall. Bobby used to give the first period of training to an English fitness coach called Roger Spry, a great guy who had worked in Brazil and was wonderful on movement and so on. Then Bobby would do the tactical stuff. It was perfect for José just to be there and take it all in. In our course for the UEFA pro licence, the most important thing is the practical work. The students must attach themselves to a club for a week and shadow the head coach. Then our tutors go and watch them and help them. José was learning that way week after week, month after month, year after year. I went over once to make a film for UEFA and could see that he was totally integrated in what Bobby was doing.

He would have learned a lot about man-management, because Bobby was brilliant at that. Then, at Barcelona, Louis van Gaal moves in. Totally different. While Bobby was what you might call a romantic of the game, Louis is highly structured, very much of the Dutch school. And José gets this whole new education in how to structure a day's training. Even better, he gets practical experience through being handed the team for matches. At half-time Louis would go into the dressing room with José, not to talk to the players but to listen to what José was telling them. Then later he'd discuss it with him. So now he'd gone way beyond the shadowing phase. He was actually managing a team – Barcelona, remember! It was like the ultimate finishing school.'

So he went back to Portugal and put it all into effect. Mourinho himself has traced his rise to international prominence back to Porto's UEFA Cup quarter-final against Panathinaikos in 2003. Having been beaten 1–0 in the home leg, his team had to go to a stadium where the Athens club had never lost in European competition. But one goal from Derlei took the match into extra time and another from the Brazilian striker won it. 'That changed the mentality of the club,' said Roxburgh. 'José felt he'd arrived and he was proved right as Porto went on to beat Celtic in the final.' After that, Roxburgh had organised a forum of his elite coaches and decided to break with tradition by inviting the finalists from the UEFA Cup as well as the Champions League. 'Both José and Martin O'Neill came and José's first contribution was amazing. Here he was, the new kid on the block, round the table in our boardroom in Switzerland with the Capellos and Lippis and Fergies and Wengers and all the other stars. 'One of the first questions was "What do you think of the silver goal?"' This was the rule whereby, if a knockout match were drawn after ninety minutes and a team led at the end of the first fifteen-minute period of extra time, the second period would be abandoned and the match end then. It has since been scrapped and the two periods of fifteen minutes restored. But Porto had won the UEFA Cup on a silver goal, scored by Derlei in the 115th minute of a final during which Henrik Larsson had twice equalised. 'There was quite a lot of debate and people like Marcello Lippi said they preferred two times fifteen minutes. José listened to it all. And then he made his contribution. "I thought it was a very, very interesting thing," he said, "to train my players to cope with that." He had nothing to say about whether it was a good or a bad rule. To him it was just another challenge. He was asked what he meant. He replied that he had told the players to imagine two different fifteen-minute scenarios. In one they were winning, the other losing. How would they handle it? Because those few minutes might be all they had to win the match. That told me everything about José as a coach. He wasn't voicing negative opinions about the rule – it was there, and he would train his players to make the most of it.' Similarly, he has been known to make his players practise *attacking* with ten against eleven – just in case they ever have a man sent off in a match they need to win.

A proverb adapted from Thomas Carlyle states that genius is an infinite capacity for taking pains, and while it might not be universally applicable in football, the career of Sir Alex Ferguson certainly evokes it. So do aspects of Mourinho's career. On the one hand, there is the occasional detractor like my friend who considers him a painter by numbers. On the other, there is a regiment of admirers such as José Manuel Capristano who, when vice-president of Benfica, initially regarded Mourinho as too inexperienced to handle the first team but was won over in a matter of weeks and exclaimed: 'That man was born to be a coach. I have never met anyone like him in my life. He thinks twenty-four hours a day.' Or Deco, who has said: 'Maybe other coaches have the same quality as Mourinho – but nobody works as hard as him.' Roxburgh recognised that reluctance to leave a stone unturned. 'I must have said it a thousand times. The guys I deal with, either the national coaches or the top club guys, are *obsessed* with detail. That's what makes them different. Louis van Gaal, for example. I remember him coming to one of our meetings – he was at Barcelona with José at the time – and complaining that, in the Champions League, the gap in time between the warm-up and the kick-off was too long. He told me to get it changed. Now, it was only a minute too long, two minutes at the most. But he was insistent. So we changed the countdown. These are tiny details. But they matter to such people. José's very much like that.'

Preparation is fundamental to Mourinho's approach. And writing things down. Anyone watching Sir Alex Ferguson would sense that here was a man who liked to live on the edge, to improvise, to rescue situations with a bold substitution (or two, as in Barcelona in 1999, when Teddy Sheringham and Ole Gunnar Solskjaer turned an impending Champions League final defeat by Bayern Munich into glorious victory). Mourinho leaves the absolute minimum to chance. 'He does have that instinct for the game,' said Roxburgh, 'but he prefers to do as much as possible through preparation. He is also very good – and this would have been honed with Van Gaal – at analysing his own team's games. José says this. You watch him in the first half of a game. He's got a little pad and he takes notes. Only in the first half. He doesn't do it in the second half. Some people like to take notes, others to use little tape recorders. Fergie, incidentally, does neither.' Ferguson, indeed, is proud of being able to carry everything in his head. 'He's got perfect recall,' said Roxburgh, 'a photographic brain – that's why he's so good at quizzes – but José likes to jot down what he calls his little reminders. By the time he goes in to see his players at half-time, he's talked to his assistants and got his talk ready so the points he wants to make can be punched out. The reason he doesn't take notes in the second half is that he's not going to speak to them at the end. He doesn't think that works. He prefers to go off and analyse it later.'

Today, with the aid of technology, coaches exchange information more than ever before. So I asked Roxburgh if, at his forums, he had noticed a certain convergence. Were the top ones becoming much of a muchness, all preaching the same dogma? Or did Mourinho's achievements mark him out as a man apart? 'It's a hard question to answer,' he said, 'but I don't think they are all alike.' There would always be differences of emphasis. 'I remember being involved in the tsunami relief match in Barcelona and our dressing room contained an array of talent beyond belief. Everywhere you looked there was a great player. You'd think that, when you get to that level, one would be as good as the other. But they've all got their own personalities and specialities. David Beckham is different from Ronaldinho. And they perform at their peak when the environment is right. If you look at coaches, Marcello Lippi's record proves he is high class – "Lippi's got us all beat," Fergie was always in the habit of saying – but when he went to Inter it didn't work. Different qualities suit different contexts. It's a matter of chemistry. José Mourinho might not be the right guy for a certain club. Yet they've all got the same tools today. They've all got these computer systems and analysts and expert advisers all around them. They've got psychologists – well, some do and some don't – and the ability to monitor their players' fitness. These things are only back-up. It's how they use the tools, how they relate the information to football players – and that's such a delicate, fragile relationship.' So what puts the best above the rest? 'They wear three hats.'

Three hats?

'Selector. Coach. Manager.'

In the past, Roxburgh explained, before the supervision of professional teams became as developed and scientific as it is today, many of the top people were good at selection and management but modest in their knowledge of training methods. 'Now look at Alex Ferguson or Arsène Wenger or José Mourinho. They wear all three hats and they wear them well. They can *select*, which means more than just picking and balancing your team. It means deciding which players to buy in order to improve your team. It means choosing your scouts – so your club can choose which players to buy and discover new talent – and the other backroom staff.

'Then there's the *coaching* hat, which entails training people to be better and gelling them into a team.

'To get the *management* hat, you have to be able to handle the players, to maintain discipline and order and so on. Certain people stand out at certain things. Fabio Capello, for instance, is brilliant on discipline. But he definitely has three hats. And there's no doubt in my mind that José has all three.' One difference between them, of course, being that while Capello began with a name,

Mourinho had to make his. But Roxburgh insists that renders Capello an exception to the rule. 'I actually think the majority of the top coaches are guys who have had to think, and work at it. Guys who have a sympathy for the learner. The ability to deliver a pass and the ability to deliver a message – these are completely different things.'

Selection

José Mourinho always had an eye for a player and a system. Otherwise his scouting reports would not have found such favour with Sir Bobby Robson, let alone satisfied Louis van Gaal, whom even his best friends would consider as fiercely demanding a coach as any on earth. And Mourinho, upon being given the opportunity, wasted little time in using his judgement. While waiting to take over at Leiria, he travelled to Brazil and came back with a couple of players, Derlei and Maciel, paying far less than they proved to be worth. At Porto, he rebuilt quickly, cheaply and to dramatic effect. But Chelsea was a different sort of challenge: the budget was huge and expectations in proportion. And what he was being asked to fix was not exactly broken because Claudio Ranieri had steered the team to second place in the Premier League and the Champions League semi-finals. Mourinho went about it in his usual businesslike way, sending Roman

Abramovich, Eugene Tenenbaum (the owner's right-hand man) and Peter Kenyon a computer presentation with lists of players he wanted to retain, discard or recruit and the infrastructure he required. (Being aware that Chelsea's scruffy training ground near Heathrow Airport had come to serve as little more than a joke among the players, he was reassured to learn that a sparkling new facility was under construction at Cobham in Surrey and would be in use within weeks.) All was agreed on Abramovich's yacht.

Already there were reports that Mourinho would be going back to Porto for three of his European champions, and at his inaugural press briefing in London, I asked if they were true. He shook his head and said there might be one signing from Porto. 'I don't need players I know,' he stressed. Englishmen such as John Terry and Frank Lampard would be relied upon as before. 'I don't need to bring in players for protection. When I was at Barcelona with Louis van Gaal, he kept bringing in Dutch players. This is something I don't want. It shows two things. That you are not so self-confident as you think – it's like a young boy who goes on holiday with his parents all the time because he is afraid to go on his own. Also that you are not such a good professional if you only know players from your own country.' It was a stirringly forthright answer: one of many that were to keep us agog through the coming months. Perhaps it would have been less well received, however, if we had realised it was utter piffle. Four of the first seven players Mourinho signed were from Portugal and it would have been five out of eight had he landed Deco, who chose to go to Barcelona instead. Even without Deco, he took two from Porto – Paulo Ferreira and Ricardo Carvalho – as well as Tiago from Benfica and the youngster Nuno Morais from Penafiel. All were represented by his own agent and confidant, Jorge Mendes, so the transfers were hardly bolts from the blue. On this occasion, Mourinho must have been reading from the wrong tin. Or maybe, as a relative newcomer to the world of wheeling and dealing, he made his error through an inadequate grasp of the art of obfuscation. He still has some difficulty (thank goodness) with that.

'When you take over a club,' said Gérard Houllier, who supervised the modernisation of Liverpool before making way for Rafael Benítez, 'you have to build and maintain three teams – the team that is playing, the team that is *not* playing and the team behind the team.'

The first team had already begun to take shape in Mourinho's mind. Carlo Cudicini was in place and Petr Čech was arriving from Rennes to challenge him. Paulo Ferreira and Ricardo Carvalho would join John Terry in a defence stiffened by the presence, just in front of the centre-backs, of Claude Makelele. The other midfield positions would be contested by Tiago, Joe Cole, Geremi and Alexei Smertin with Damien Duff and the most exciting of the new boys Kenyon had secured in advance,

Arjen Robben, supplying width. Eidur Gudjohnsen would play a little off the front. Behind Hernan Crespo. The Argentine, though, was to be the subject of a joint reappraisal. When the players reported for duty at the old Imperial College training ground, Crespo was a notable and unexplained exception. When they were handed Mourinho's guide to behaviour and ethos, the copy intended for Crespo went unclaimed. 'From here, each practice, each game, each minute of your social life must centre on the aim of being champions,' it read, ending with a line that might have come from Lord Kitchener: 'I need all of you.' Two days later, Crespo strolled in from South America, mumbling excuses about flights. He was called into Mourinho's office, given a vibrant lecture and asked if he would settle in England and give the same commitment as the rest of the players. He declined and was loaned to Milan, though Crespo was to return in time for the 2005–06 season. And Chelsea promptly smashed their transfer record in paying Olympique Marseille £24 million for his replacement, Didier Drogba.

The non-playing team, the group of players on the fringes who would have to be kept motivated during spells of inactivity, Mourinho addressed with a clear-out. The last thing a coach needs is malcontents. But sometimes the cost of getting rid of such players when they are in mid-contract can be daunting. Mourinho was lucky. His club could afford to pay them off. Crespo was a good example in the sense that, with wages in Italy under sharp downward pressure, Milan were unwilling to contemplate paying his salary of £4.8 million for the year. So Chelsea gave them two-thirds of it. (Had Chelsea reached the Champions League final, they would have been paying him twice as much as Milan – to play against them.) They had already shipped Juan Sebastián Verón to Inter in a similar loan deal. Off to Birmingham City on permanent transfers went Mario Melchiot and Jesper Gronkjaer. Middlesbrough took Jimmy Floyd Hasselbaink. With retirements and less significant departures, the squad was cut to what Mourinho considered a manageable size: twenty-three senior players. Given that two or three of these would be injured most of the time, the potential for grumbling would be minimal. And Mourinho would be working only with players who had a reasonable chance of contributing to matches, even in a small way; there would be no clutter, no wastage of effort, and that is exactly the environment in which Mourinho likes to coach.

As for the team behind the team – as Houllier referred to the back-up staff – Mourinho had already assembled most of them. He began to form his inner circle of assistants while preparing to go to Leiria. Although only too eager to test his 'methodology' after a somewhat false start to his solo career at Benfica, he sensed a requirement for an enforcer, someone who could deal with the players. His wife suggested Baltemar Brito, and Mourinho was to work with him for many years. He was more than an assistant; Brito was a close friend. They had known each other since the Brazilian – a tall and bow-legged central defender, gritty and reliable but of limited technique – played for Mourinho's father at Rio Ave in 1981–82; José, remember, was a junior member of that squad. Brito was joint 'assistant manager' at Chelsea. But some assistant managers are more equal than others and Brito, rather than Stevie Clarke, seemed to take charge when Mourinho was unavoidably absent from the bench during Chelsea's Champions League run. Clarke, though, was clearly accepted into Mourinho's group. The former Chelsea defender, a Scot, was one of few surviving connections with the past and his initial function was to point Mourinho to areas which had been neglected under the Ranieri regime, such as youth development. He was the ideal link man and went on to work with Gianfranco Zola at West Ham United and Kenny Dalglish at Liverpool.

Then there was Rui Faria, the fitness coach whom Mourinho inadvertently exposed to ridicule during the Bayern Munich matches by appearing to use him to pass messages and, in Germany, face the press; one columnist referred to him as 'puerile', another called him a 'woolly-hatted halfwit'. He is the longest-serving member of Mourinho's circle. When Mourinho was assisting Louis van Gaal at Barcelona, a student from the sports university in Porto got in touch, seeking help in completing his final papers. How could Mourinho, himself a graduate of the corresponding establishment in Lisbon, refuse? They got on so well, furthermore, that when Mourinho joined Leiria, the former student, Rui Faria, was beckoned.

Silvino Louro looked after the Chelsea goalkeepers, as he had done those of Porto; Mourinho found him there when he arrived from Leiria. Setúbal-born, Silvino had the most distinguished playing career of the group. He played twenty-three times for Portugal in goal and twice appeared for Benfica in European Champions' Cup finals: in 1988, when PSV Eindhoven beat them on penalties and Hans van Breukelen, his opposite number, was the hero; and in 1990, when, coached by Sven-Göran Eriksson, they lost to a Milan goal scored by Frank Rijkaard. Like Rui Faria, Silvino followed Mourinho to Internazionale and on to Real Madrid.

André Villas-Boas, when working under Mourinho at Chelsea, had the title 'assistant coach/scout' and an air of mystery that transcended it. At Porto he was called something like 'director of opposition intelligence'. Villas-Boas was Mourinho's spy. He watched and analysed opponents, just as Mourinho had done for others, and prepared dossiers to be handed to the players, normally twenty-four hours before matches. He too dealt in detail, supplying rundowns on each possible opponent, including what kind of runs the player liked to make, whether he favoured the left or right side, whether he liked to dribble or pass, his stamina levels, capabilities in the air and temperament. Another thing Villas-Boas had in common with the young Mourinho was that he aspired to be a head coach; not long after coming to London, he happened to mention it in public. Mourinho was not pleased and told Villas-Boas to stop speaking to the press. Perhaps it was just as well. Publicity and intelligence work can be strange bedfellows.

A quick glance at an internet site containing a brief biography of Villas-Boas, however, led us to the information that he had a British grandmother – not unusual in Oporto, due to the port trade – and coached youths at Porto before turning up as technical director of the British Virgin Islands FA in 1999 . . . when he was twenty-one! Sir Bobby Robson remembered him at Porto. He was in his teens when Robson was coach there and used to wait outside the Englishman's apartment. At first the boy wanted just an autograph or a chat and Robson obliged. But when he asked for a job on the Porto staff, the response could only be a gentle refusal. Villas-Boas wrote to Robson at Barcelona, repeating his request for a start in the game. He must also have kept in touch with Mourinho, for when Mourinho took charge at Porto, he turned up on the staff, ready to follow in his footsteps. He, too, was a good analyst. Just as Robson and Van Gaal trusted Mourinho, Mourinho trusted Villas-Boas. Maybe the British Virgin Islands job came too soon for him. He is remembered there also. The president of the British Virgin Islands FA between 1996 and 2000, Kenrick Grant, told me: 'His plans were very impressive on paper and so we gave him a job as youth director and assistant to our head coach on 350 US dollars a week plus expenses. But he was always very quiet. He'd had the privilege to be around the top people in Portugal, apparently, and never really settled or got focused here. Whenever he had the opportunity, he'd go back to Portugal. One time, he wrote to me asking for a reference and I said I was sorry but I could not do that. He never came back to us. I was really surprised to hear he was with a top team like Chelsea.'

Not for nothing was Villas-Boas called 'Mini-Mourinho' before he struck out on his own so successfully. When his erstwhile master was feuding with Frank Rijkaard, the pupil took a prominent role.

Imagine Kenrick Grant's astonishment when Villas-Boas was called back to Stamford Bridge as team boss in the summer of 2011. Amid the euphoric scenes as Stamford Bridge prepared for Pierluigi Collina to blow the final whistle on Chelsea's victory over Barcelona, Villas-Boas swaggered towards the visitors' dugout and said something that irked Rijkaard, whom a steward restrained. As the Barcelona players trooped off, Villas-Boas was still apparently taunting them and Samuel Eto'o motioned to him to shut up. As again a steward intervened, bundling Eto'o away, Villas-Boas stood triumphant, sneering. It was not an edifying sight.

Villas-Boas remained a member of the Mourinho coterie until the end of the first Inter season, 2008–09, when he decided to pursue his ambition to be the number one

at a club (again just like Mourinho). Soon he was engaged by Academica of Coimbra, who lay at the bottom
of Portugal's first division. He lifted them into mid-table
and, in the summer of 2010, followed in Mourinho's footsteps once more by taking over at Porto. Immediately
they beat Benfica in the Supercup, Portugal's equivalent
of the Community Shield, and by 3 April 2011 they were
champions, making sure of the title with a 2–1 triumph
over Benfica in Lisbon. The comparison with Mourinho's
time at Porto became increasingly uncanny as they went
on to win the Europa League. And then he too was called
by Abramovich to the Bridge.

In Mourinho's time at Chelsea, all of his assistants,
from the unassuming Brito to young Villas-Boas, had to
be treated respectfully by the Bridge players. Mourinho,
who was afforded the same courtesy by Van Gaal at
Barcelona, insisted on it. The first commandment of
Mourinho's 'bible', the document hidden in his laptop
which set out his coaching principles, apparently laid
down that no individual must be greater than the club (a
tenet which any benevolent dictator would find convenient) and the team behind the team had their own status.
Each member was there because Mourinho felt he could
trust him. Trust was fundamental to what he called his
'methodology'. But upon arriving at Chelsea he needed
to be able to trust his lieutenant on the field more than
anyone and so his choice of captain was a key decision.

Under Ranieri the role had been taken by Marcel

Desailly, with John Terry deputising when the great but somewhat creaky French defender was taking one of his frequent rests (Desailly retired just before Mourinho's arrival). When Chelsea flew to the United States for their pre-season tour, Terry was only twenty-three but an established member of the England squad who had taken the suspended Rio Ferdinand's place alongside Sol Campbell in Sven-Göran Eriksson's defence during the European Championship and done well. But Mourinho's initial instinct was that Frank Lampard, whom he considered a more intelligent footballer, should be his captain. During the flight across the Atlantic, however, he consulted the players one by one and a consensus emerged that Terry should have the armband. Mourinho went to sit next to Terry on the plane and the choice was confirmed. 'He told me what he wanted from me as captain,' said Terry. 'He told me that, on the training pitch and around the place, he wanted me to be a speaker and out there in games he wanted me to get his words across to the players.' The consequences of that decision were long to echo around a united, vibrant dressing room; Mourinho had listened to its voice and picked just the man, and towards the end of the season players up and down the country recognised it by choosing Terry as the Professional Footballers' Association Player of the Year.

So, having selected a lean squad with a strong leader, Mourinho needed to choose the right tactical framework for them. At Porto he had favoured a tight midfield diamond: in other words, 4–4–2 without wingers. At least that was what he had shown us in the Champions League, when Porto were often facing teams such as Real Madrid or Manchester United who had more players of outstanding individual accomplishment; he would some-times use a different formation against inferior sides in Portugal. The requirement to switch for the Champions League he explained thus: 'To win we had to go about things in a certain way. If you have a Ferrari and I have a small car, to beat you in a race I have to break your wheel or put sugar in your tank.'

At Chelsea, initially, he appeared still to be suffering from small-car syndrome. 'They started with a diamond and people were saying they were a bit dour,' recalled David Moyes, whose Everton lost each of their matches to Chelsea 1–0. After nine Premier League fixtures, Mourinho's team had scored a mere eight goals. But they were without Arjen Robben and his arrival on the scene, belated due to the first of his injuries, changed everything. In their next nine matches, they scored twenty-nine goals and developed a new system. 'I don't know if he stumbled on it or what,' said Moyes, 'but good managers do that. They find a system that suits their players and, when Robben came into a side that already had Damien Duff, they had two top-class wide players. So Mourinho developed this version of 4–3–3.'

Whatever circumstances called for, he would supply, notably in the Champions League: against Barcelona, lightning-quick counter-attacking; against Bayern, long high balls towards Didier Drogba, an old-fashioned English centre-forward who happened to come from the Ivory Coast. In the Premier League, one memorable act of boldness occurred in the west London derby with Fulham, who were drawing at Stamford Bridge when Mourinho threw on Robben and moved Duff to left-back, which meant Chelsea had no fewer than six attackers on the field. There were, moreover, forty-five minutes to go. But fewer than ten of those minutes had passed when Duff surged forward and prompted Robben, whose perfectly laid ball Frank Lampard stroked into the net. Mourinho then adjusted the balance of the team again, replacing Drogba with the midfielder Tiago, and Chelsea won 3–1.

In Ranieri's day this had been called tinkering; now it was tactical acumen. Only against Liverpool at what proved the end of Mourinho's Champions League campaign did he fail to come up with a solution to Chelsea's difficulties, which were probably due to mental bluntness as much as anything else, the second leg having fallen three days after the Premier League had been clinched at Bolton. What he could choose he chose wisely. But he could not always pick his moments.

Coaching

David Moyes suddenly grinned. 'What Mourinho's done,' said the Everton manager, 'is make coaching sexy.' He was alluding less to his rival's good looks than to a tendency to use fancy words and phrases to describe his methods. One of these is 'guided discovery', by which Mourinho means that players at a certain level must be led gently to lessons rather than told what to do; it is an approach he learned at Barcelona, one he shares with, among others, Sven-Göran Eriksson. On the other hand, we heard from John Terry, he was not above barking to his Chelsea charges: 'Hey – don't fuck about!'

In an interview with Andy Roxburgh for UEFA's coaching magazine soon after he joined Chelsea, Mourinho described his coaching style as flexible and evolutionary – 'I am different today from five years ago' – but very demanding in terms of the commitment required from the players during training. 'I have always been lucky to have more than one pitch at my training centre,' he said, 'and I therefore prepare my sessions in such a way that I can jump from one situation to another with effective working time high and resting time very low. We go for quality and high intensity during short periods. Players want to work, whether it is in Portugal, England or Spain, as long as the training is well organised and serious and they know the purpose of the exercise.

'When I went to Scotland in the late 1980s, after finishing my studies, your methods [he told Roxburgh] made me think about methodology in a different way. The way you used small-sided games to develop technical, tactical and fitness training – a global view of training. I believe in the global method. My fitness coach works with me on the tactical systems, advising on time, distance and space. I want to develop tactical aspects of the game: how to press, when to press, transitions, ball possession, positional play. After that other things come – the physical and psychological aspects are part of the exercise. The individual work is done when we feel the players need that. Often we need to separate the players into groups depending on their condition and the amount of playing time they have had. The emphasis of the work is always tactical.'

It's not always so sexy, then, but the Chelsea players did swear that they loved their briskly conducted work with Mourinho and, by his side, Rui Faria. And, while there was no shortage of public testimony – 'training is enjoyable every day,' said John Terry, 'and you learn so much' – the best evidence was what they said privately. As the anecdotal evidence built up over Mourinho's first season, the former Arsenal striker Ian Wright said he had been told even the players on the fringe of the first team enjoyed training – 'and that is a major achievement'. Meanwhile Gérard Houllier, whose post-Liverpool role as expert analyst of English football on French television kept him in touch with the Premier League grapevine, told me: 'Believe me – the players just love Mourinho's coaching and man-management.' The two linked together, of course, in accordance with the global principle.

In Tel Aviv, Mourinho told his audience: 'A great pianist doesn't run around the piano or do push-ups with the tips of his fingers. To be great, he plays the piano. He plays all his life and being a great footballer is not about running, push-ups or physical work generally. The best way to be a great player is to play football.' That said, he added, a good coach must know more than football. 'He has to be a leader of men and a coherent leader. He must make all his men feel big, not small.' A compact squad is helpful in this context.

The influence of Louis van Gaal at Barcelona was clear from Mourinho's tactical syllabus – possession and positional play had always been central pillars of the Van Gaal method – but the Dutchman had noted a divergence on philosophy. 'He has more belief in defence than attack,' said Van Gaal. 'My philosophy is always – because I believe we must entertain the public – to have attacking play. *His philosophy is to win!* That is the difference.' And in 2010, when Mourinho's Inter beat Van Gaal's Bayern Munich in the Champions League final in Madrid, it was Mourinho who won. But nothing Van Gaal had said about his former pupil was to brand Mourinho a philistine. Mourinho had gone out of his way to deny that, for all his belief in match analysis and preparatory work, he saw football as a science rather than an art; like most coaches, he considered the game a combination of the two. But he had, it was true, no time for unnecessary embellishment, and a much-lauded example of his individual coaching when at Chelsea was his trimming of those fussy frills from the game of Joe Cole, who emerged from the process a regular and productive member of the England team, until injury dimmed his light.

In Mourinho's first few months at Chelsea, he was often exasperated by Cole and his tricks. An erstwhile boy wonder at West Ham, the Londoner seemed perpetually to be trying to vindicate his early publicity, which had hailed him as a new George Best, an English answer to Diego Maradona, and all the rest of the usual suspect theories. What Cole usually turned out to be was a very gifted midfield technician with a limited understanding of the necessity to play in a team context. It was not that he lacked will, but that he misapplied it and had a tendency to lose concentration. Chelsea had paid nearly £7 million for him in the summer of 2003, but Cole could not persuade Claudio Ranieri to establish him in the team; he made half of his appearances for the Italian as a substitute. Mourinho, having cleared out some of Cole's competition in the creativity department – notably Juan Sebastián Verón – and been deprived of the unfortunate Scott Parker through injury, gave Cole some opportunities, but he soon lost his place to Damien Duff and in early October, after he had come off the bench to score the only goal of a home match with Liverpool, Mourinho alluded to the reasons: 'After he scored, the game finished for Joe. I need eleven players for defensive organisation and I had just ten. Joe had two faces – one beautiful and another which I did not like.'

Nearly six months later, Cole was picked to start a World Cup qualifying match against Northern Ireland at Old Trafford. England won 4–0 and Cole, having scored the first goal in some style, shaking off a challenge and sending a controlled drive into Maik Taylor's left-hand corner, performed with impressive maturity. 'He has finally learned,' said Sven-Göran Eriksson, 'that football is not about making tricks – it's about knowing when to do it. Today I don't think he ever lost the ball in a stupid position, which was his problem in the past. He showed he can beat people – you want him to do that – but also keep it simple, and he showed he can defend.' Cole had, in short, completed the journey from stage act to international footballer and he was not backward in thanking Mourinho. 'He's the first person to really look at me and my game,' declared Cole. 'I can genuinely say he's had a massive influence on my career. I listen to him – he's a European champion.' And the public admonition after the Liverpool match had had its effect. 'Something like that can ram the nail home and I know what I've got to do now. His criticism is always constructive. He'll always sit me down and talk about my game and what he wants me to do. He's so advanced with the tactical stuff and he's made me really think about that side of things. There's been a steady improvement and I can become even better.'

Deco was another beneficiary of Mourinho's guide to self-discovery. It occurred to me during the latter stages of Porto's successful Champions League run that here was a team so disciplined as to bear comparison with the Milan founded by Arrigo Sacchi or – the search for another example ended closer to home – George Graham's Arsenal. Just as those teams were leavened by highly creative players, Mourinho acknowledged the necessity for flair by having Deco as a key man. For all his gifts, though, Deco did not just wait for the ball to come to him; he worked and probed and challenged until the openings came. In short, he was – to use a favourite word of Graham's – productive. 'Mourinho is special,' Deco has said, 'because he is one of the few people capable of changing a player's mentality. He didn't change the way I play – he improved it. He got me thinking a lot more.' Deco, who was born and raised in Brazil, developed so well under Mourinho that he was encouraged to take Portuguese nationality. He made his debut for his adopted country shortly before the UEFA Cup final in 2003. It was at home against Brazil – and he scored the only goal. Much of Deco's life had resembled a fairy tale; he even recovered from the disappointment of Barcelona's defeat at Chelsea to collect a Spanish championship at the climax of his first season at the Camp Nou.

Another player of talent was Abdelsatar Sabry, an Egyptian known simply as Sabry in Portugal. He was at Benfica when Mourinho arrived in September 2000 and popular with the fans. Although skilled and with a knack of scoring in big matches, Sabry had no sense of team play. He was like an unreformed Joe Cole, only more so. He objected to Mourinho's use of him on the left flank and, what was more, told a newspaper as much; he said he wanted a free role behind the main striker. Mourinho responded in public. He said Sabry kept giving the ball away and cited a derby against Belenenses in which he lost possession so often that, at one stage, Benfica were counter-attacked five times in sixteen minutes. 'A number-ten player,' Mourinho continued, referring to the playmaker's role, the Deco role, 'must display a high tactical level in order to be a link between the defence and attack – *but not the defence and attack of the opponent.*' As if this were not a devastating enough dismissal of Sabry's analysis of his own worth, Mourinho added that he was forever being caught offside. Oh, and he wasn't scoring enough goals. As events were to transpire, Mourinho went and Sabry stayed, at least for a while. Two years later, when Mourinho was at Porto and a burgeoning Deco about to take the international stage, Sabry was at Estrela da Amadora, with little to celebrate but the favourable verdict of a court on his demand that Benfica stump up more than £200,000 in unpaid wages.

Mourinho has never been interested in players who are reluctant to learn and the quality of those he coached at Chelsea helped to produce swift results. Even in the Carling Cup final, one of his beliefs was effectively enacted. Earlier in the season, Scott Parker had alluded to it when he said: 'We are doing a lot more ball work, playing keep-ball.' This was to do with Mourinho's concept of 'resting on the ball', which he has described as 'keeping possession for the sake of possession' on the grounds that it is safer to rest when your team, rather than the opposition, have the ball. When he was at Porto, an opposing coach complimented Mourinho after a match by saying his players had never come off the field so tired. Chelsea used the ploy in making Liverpool chase for long periods in Cardiff and afterwards Terry said: 'We saw their legs go.'

Against Barcelona in the Champions League, the work Chelsea did on both aspects of 'transitions' (counter-attacking) was manifest. Mourinho, asked by Andy Roxburgh which trends he had noticed in the contemporary game, replied: 'Transitions have become crucial.

When the opponent is organised defensively, it is very difficult to score. The moment the opponent loses the ball can be the time to exploit the opportunity of someone being out of position. Similarly, when we lose the ball, we must react immediately. In training I sometimes practise keeping a minimum of five players behind the ball, so that when we lose it we can still keep a good defensive shape. The players must learn to read the game – when to press and when to get back to their defensive positions. Everybody says that set plays win most games, but I think it is more about transitions.'

Mourinho would have appreciated something David Moyes said about Chelsea: 'They're a clever team.' The Everton coach was referring to the match between the clubs at Goodison Park in February, when Everton's James Beattie was sent off early for butting William Gallas. 'It was interesting,' said Moyes. 'We couldn't get the ball from them. They wouldn't let it out of play and they didn't concede free-kicks. We were doing everything we could to find a way of restarting the game with a throw or a corner or a free-kick so we could make it a scrap for the ball. With ten men, it would have been our best opportunity. They didn't give us it and I remember thinking what an intelligent team they were.' There was something else Mourinho did that day which Moyes, when I told him about it, thought clever. But it was more in the way of management than coaching, so we shall save it for a moment. They do, though, blend into each other, coaching and management.

Infectious, isn't it, this global spirit?

Management

That day at Everton had presented Mourinho with a problem. Chelsea had led the Premier League for three months – since they beat Everton at Stamford Bridge – and although Arsenal had yet to recover the form that their Old Trafford experience had disrupted, Manchester United were challenging. Chelsea went to Merseyside with a nine-point advantage. United had a derby against Manchester City the following day. The dismissal of James Beattie seemed just what Chelsea would have wanted, but breaching a depleted team is not always easy, as Mourinho told us. He was responding to someone who asked, before the trip to Barcelona, if it were not a comfort at such times to be sitting on a cushion at the top of one's domestic league. He smiled ruefully. 'Maybe you won't believe this,' he said, 'but towards the end of the first half at Everton, between the thirtieth and forty-fifth minutes, I felt the players were too anxious to score against ten men and lost their shape.' Having devised a means of relieving them of their obligation, he strode to the dressing room. 'I told them to let the game flow, because a point would be good, no problem. "If we drop two points," I said, "we stay seven points clear, even if Manchester United win tomorrow. So there's no pressure. Now let's go." I didn't make any changes. I didn't scream at them. I just reminded them of those nine points and said, "If we score, we score. If we don't score, we don't score."' He paused slightly. *'I was desperate to score!'* Eidur Gudjohnsen obliged and Chelsea had three more points. United, though they won at the City of Manchester Stadium, realised – because that weekend, given the status Everton had acquired, had been seen as a milestone – they were fighting for second place. What did Moyes, now he had been apprised of Mourinho's team-talk, think of it? 'Great management.'

Management has always been to do with psychology. And Mourinho has never been above playing the odd trick on his own men. A few days before what turned out to be his last match with Benfica – the derby against Sporting – he decided to indulge his affection for tennis at the Masters Cup, which was being held in Lisbon that year. He went with his assistant, Carlos Mozer, and, having spotted the Sporting players strolling among the throng of spectators, resolved to turn this to his advantage. He told Mozer he was going to 'poison' his own team by telling them the Sporting players were obviously so confident of thrashing Benfica they had neglected to prepare for the match in favour of disporting themselves all week at the tennis. He was, of course, exaggerating wildly and later confessed to it; he had simply been spinning the tale in order to put an additional edge on his own players' appetites for the derby, which they won 3–0.

No slight, real or imagined, is ever wasted. Most coaches do this but few have done it as effectively as Mourinho. Sir Alex Ferguson is a great exponent. In the Scot's first big job, at Aberdeen, he used the city's relative isolation from Glasgow, where the 'Old Firm' of Rangers and Celtic had traditionally ruled the game, to build a stockade mentality, and he contrived to do much the same at Manchester United, even though the club was the best supported in the land; the players were led to believe that everyone, including those in authority in the game, was out to get them or at least desperate to see them fail. When he and Mourinho faced each other in the Champions League, they were two of a kind. Mourinho, once Chelsea had all but taken the English title, admitted to using similar tactics. Or almost admitted it. What he said was that there had been a 'psychological fight' against critics who had called his team 'boring' in the opening weeks of the season. 'Maybe the criticism made us stronger. We had to close the shell. We created something strong inside. We went through that period and then a beautiful period.' And, once on top, they had remained strong. 'We always look at newspapers and TV and every day there was a headline saying Chelsea will have a blip, Arsenal will come back, United will shock them, Chelsea will lose points in the north, Chelsea will lose points in the south. All season! We needed to be strong.' I imagined him staying up all night in the team hotel, prowling the corridors when the newspapers came round and carefully cutting out all the complimentary bits before they could read them and go weak at the knees.

The most unusual facet of Mourinho's management also pertains to his bonding technique. Scorning the convention that even the kindest coach must maintain a certain distance between himself and the players, he actually behaves like one of them, a sort of twelfth man. It was especially noticeable when he was at Chelsea. He celebrated victory over Barcelona by running on to the pitch, roaring and wheeling his right arm, with the fist clenched, so that the tail of the famous grey overcoat fluttered; lest it be thought he had succumbed to total abandon, however, I should add that he kept a firmly restraining left hand on the pocket containing his mobile phone. Then Mourinho jumped player-style on the broad back of his captain, John Terry. It was that great observer of the human race (and inveterate football follower) Desmond Morris who drew my attention to it. 'I cannot think of another manager who could have got away with that,' he added. 'If Big Ron Atkinson had tried it, he'd probably have broken the poor lad's back!' But Morris had a point to make. 'Both of Mourinho's legs were off the ground. It was a piece of body language I've never seen in football before. It means he's one of the players.' What's more, his participation in some of Chelsea's wildest celebrations seemed perfectly natural in the context of that particular man and those players. As Ian Wright put it: 'If another manager hugged his players, they might be sort of rigid, cringing, embarrassed. But you can see the camaraderie between him and the team. There is a deep respect there. You can see that they really love him.'

Love?

I thought that might be a bit strong. So I decided to ask a less excitable, more seasoned footballing figure for his impression. 'No,' said Gérard Houllier, 'it's true. He has this kind of complicity with the players. They don't just like José. They love him.' And he loves them, as you can see from his post-match tours. And they love each other, which became increasingly apparent during the march to the title when kisses were commonly exchanged.

In the match programme for the home leg of the Champions League tie against Liverpool there is a picture of Claude Makelele, his face obscured by the enveloping arms of Terry, who is leaning down and planting an earnest smacker on the top of his head; Makelele has his left arm wrapped tightly round the captain's waist. Players do that kind of thing. But usually they do it with a grin. Although at Mourinho's Chelsea some demonstrations of affection flirted with the outer fringes of the faintly nauseating, they did, I confess, also stir feelings of wonder at how it must be on the inside of such a passionate scrum, especially while everything is being carried before it. These players had been led to believe in each other and throughout the 2004–05 season, courtesy of Sky television's access to the pre-match tunnel, we could see Terry glance over his shoulder at colleagues who clearly shared his conviction that they could not lose. The central significance of Terry's relationship with Mourinho to the events of the season was undeniable and in March the captain declared: 'Every result is for the manager. He works so hard, him and his staff. On the pitch all of us fight for each other but deep down it's for him. He's the best, we believe he's the best and we're lucky to have him. Everything about the man is first class.'

Mourinho went about the job of unifying the Chelsea dressing room straight away. Cliques were out, he told the press quite bluntly: 'You go to some places and maybe you find an English corner, a French corner and, at some clubs, a black corner. I don't like any of that. It cannot work.' There would be a common language: 'If you are on my table for breakfast and I keep speaking Portuguese, you turn round and say, "Sorry, fuck off, I don't sit at your table any more." The language has to be English. If they don't speak it fluently when they come, they must study.' They soon discovered one reason why. Mourinho announced that the final team-talk before matches would be given not by him but by a player. Before the Bayern

Munich matches, when Mourinho was suspended, the young German defender Robert Huth said: 'We have a meeting with him two hours before a game and after that everybody is left to themselves because we all have different ways to prepare. Then we go for the warm-up, but it's not like the coach has a big final word. He leaves it up to one of us to give the rallying call. We choose the player on the day.' By 'we' he meant the players and staff: often Stevie Clarke made the final decision.

Mourinho informed them they were unbeatable and should never forget it, because successful teams had no fear of losing. The allure of such meaningless statements, usually purloined from the writings of American sports coaches, escapes many outsiders, but it is rarely lost on players. Chelsea's were told that Porto had been fearless and that, given Porto's achievements, was good enough for them. When the Champions League pitted them against Barcelona, said Terry: 'Initially you think "great side", which they are, but when you've got a manager drumming it into you every day that you are the best, that there isn't going to be anybody better, it rubs off on the players and we go out there believing it.' Lampard added that Mourinho had the knack of being able to transmit his 'amazing confidence' to every player.

He has an almost quaint liking for pen and paper. Everything he has done in his coaching career, from day one with the youths at Vitória Setúbal, has been written in notebooks and retained. This is not unique.

Everton's David Moyes told me: 'I've written down what every coach I've ever worked with has done – with my own ideas alongside, such as "I wouldn't have put the centre-half in here" or whatever. Even now, my assistant [Alan Irvine at the time] writes down everything we do at Everton – I could tell you what our training routines were three years ago last Thursday! But José, as I say, somehow manages to make it sound sexy.'

His habit of getting substitutes to carry on written messages to other players fascinated Portuguese viewers; the cameras would zoom in to try to sneak a look. He continued the habit in England and, after Jiří Jarošík had carried on written instructions for Tiago at Everton, the referees' overseer, Keith Hackett, was asked if regulations allowed it. 'Yes,' said an amused Hackett. 'There is nothing in the laws to prevent it. It might be different if the substitute took a Christmas hamper on to the pitch.' As always with Mourinho, however, these billets-doux have a serious purpose. Asked about the illustrated tutorial Dmitri Alenitchev was given before taking the field in Porto's Champions League final, Roxburgh said: 'José's clever enough to know which players can absorb words and which need to be shown things visually.'

To call him a hands-on coach would be understating it. While serving one of his dugout bans in Portugal, where a suspended coach is allowed to speak to his players at half-time, he was stopped on a landing by a security guard at the stadium of Porto's local rivals, Boavista, but simply picked up his mobile phone; the players heard his reassuring voice on a speaker-phone one of his assistants had taken the precaution of carrying into the dressing room. When he was banned from the second leg of the UEFA Cup semi-final against Lazio in Rome, he texted messages to the bench. One translates as 'Tell Deco I'm pissed off – I want more', another as 'Pressure on linesman, everybody'. While the latter confirms Mourinho is a psychological warrior, it is almost standard coaching practice to order your players to chip away at match officials in the hope of obtaining a marginal decision sooner or later. What set him somewhat apart was his foray from the dugout physically to prevent the Lazio player Lucas Castromán from taking a quick throw in the UEFA Cup semi-final first leg (which Porto won 4–1). For that he incurred the suspension in Rome (there the match ended 0–0) and Roxburgh, recalling how hard it hit him, could not quite suppress a laugh. 'José came to one of our UEFA meetings some time later and it clearly still rankled. Not the red card. "I deserved that," he said. "The referee was absolutely right. I had no excuse for what I did." Because one thing all these guys are is brutally honest with themselves. But José went on to say it was an absolute disgrace that, as well as denying him a seat in the dugout, they would not let him in the dressing room at half-time. He was raging about it. A lot of the others – Fergie and Wenger and people like that – were listening and some were nodding and thinking maybe he had a point. And naturally coaches are going to think that. So I took it up with UEFA. But they think a banned coach should be banned from doing any coaching at a match.' While Mourinho might have seemed to have lost the argument, his antics during his next ban, over the two legs of Chelsea's encounter with Bayern, emphasised his reluctance to accept defeat.

Mourinho's handling of players had changed. While at Benfica there were Sabry, for whom fate had disappointment in store, and Maniche, who played up in training, was banished to the reserves but two weeks later became club captain and ended up one of Mourinho's European champions at Porto. But you hardly ever heard the crack of a whip around Chelsea's training ground, at least not on the players' backs. There, the boss was almost one of the lads. While they were lacing their boots, he told funny stories of occurrences in his career, much as a player would. When he had to be tough, he would be, as in the case of Adrian Mutu, but the distance another coach would keep between himself and his charges was not observed. On the field, it was a similar story, and when they celebrated at the end of a match, a stranger would be able to tell him from Tiago and the others only through the realisation that an on-duty player would not be wearing a cashmere coat.

According to Desmond Morris, the phenomenon is linked to football's evolution. Morris and football go back a long way. The author of *The Naked Ape, The*

Human Zoo and a dozen other popular studies of man and other animals, he has been watching the game for more than seventy years and was a director of Oxford United during their rise (funded by Robert Maxwell) to the top division in the eighties. 'There was a time,' he said, 'when the captain was an important figure. In modern football, his role has become all but non-existent and the manager has taken over, leading the team and connecting it to the public through television, radio and other media, generally representing it. The manager has become a performer and the good manager will always support his team. Mourinho, though, identifies with his team more than any other manager. He is passionately involved with them. In his imagination, he is out there with them. He really is the twelfth man. As for keeping a distance, he doesn't feel a need to do it. He gets on the pitch and celebrates with them and that is what makes him different. You couldn't envisage Alex Ferguson jumping on a player's back. Or Arsène Wenger. That's why I disagree slightly with the portrayal of Mourinho as a father figure to his players. He is more like an elder brother. Or the leader of the gang.'

There was, nevertheless, an element of awe in the players' perception of Mourinho. 'He jokes with everyone,' said Frank Lampard, 'but at the same time you're a little bit wary of him.' Perhaps they sensed what Roxburgh always discerned behind his charismatic façade: a willingness to make ruthless decisions. 'It's one of the elements of management,' said Roxburgh. 'Fergie has always had it. He can like you as a person but make a decision that hurts you.' In Ferguson's case, the mind usually travels back in time to the dropping of Jim Leighton, who, after keeping goal more than reliably for Aberdeen throughout their greatest years, followed Ferguson to Manchester United and, having performed unconvincingly in the 1990 FA Cup final against Crystal Palace, a 3–3 draw, lost his place for the replay five days later; United won 1–0 and Leighton's career entered the doldrums (though, having returned to Scotland, he revived it and even became his country's oldest international at forty). Mourinho, too, could separate his human feelings from the cause of the team, said Roxburgh, and we could expect to see that if anyone repeated Adrian Mutu's error in letting him down. Might this ruthlessness, also evident in the rapid rebuilding of Porto, have been picked up from Louis van Gaal, the man who dropped Rivaldo? 'It's intrinsic,' said Roxburgh. 'It might have been lent emphasis by the time he spent with Louis, but I think it was already there inside him.'

The most exciting part of management calls for tough decisions to be made very quickly. It is the bit we see: the match. Sir Bobby Robson has a story about that and he told it at one of Roxburgh's UEFA gatherings. 'It was in Barcelona several years ago,' said Roxburgh. 'We had our fifty-two coaches from fifty-two countries and Bobby was giving a lecture on crisis management. He was talking about a time when his Barcelona side were getting whacked 3–0 at home and the white hankies were up and the whole bit. We were showing clips from the game as the goals went in and saying, "What were you thinking now, Bobby?" and Bobby replied, "At that point, I was thinking about a taxi." And then, having pulled two goals back early in the second half, they let in another. When we asked Bobby what he was thinking then, I remember Rinus Michels in the front row shouting, "Get that taxi!" And yet Barcelona won the game. José was beside Bobby in the dugout and I thought back to it when I watched José send on three substitutes at half-time when Chelsea were losing at Newcastle in the FA Cup.' So did Robson.

Let him take up the tale of that Barcelona match. 'It was against Atlético Madrid in the Cup and that, in Spain, means war. The capital against Catalunya. Whether it's Real or Atlético, it matters to our crowd. So when we go 3–0 down the hankies start fluttering. I nudged my assistant. "José," I said. "It's snowing." I had a look across the pitch and formed an idea. I didn't like the way Laurent Blanc was playing and I didn't think much of Gica Popescu either. So both of those central defenders were candidates to come off. I thought I'd do that – even though Popescu was our captain and there were still several minutes to go to the interval – and replace them with attacking players, people who might get us goals. After all, what did we have to lose? The only way we could save the game was by going forward.' A measure of defensive capability would still be provided by Abelardo, Sergi and Fernando Couto. 'I remember telling José what I was going to do and asking what he thought about it. "You've got no option, Mister," he replied. "Do it."' Blanc and Popescu were called to the bench together and Hristo Stoichkov and Juan Antonio Pizzi took the field. Within five minutes of the resumption, Ronaldo and Iván de la Pena had struck. Atlético's Milinko Pantic retaliated by completing his hat-trick. 'A bloody soft goal,' said Robson, recalling a blunder by his Portuguese goalkeeper, Vítor Baía, who was later to become a European champion under Mourinho at Porto. 'Anyway, that's us 4–2 down. Then we scored three! Figo, Ronaldo and finally Pizzi. So we won 5–4. And we were still going like pistons at the end. Another twenty minutes and we'd have won 8–4. There were some stunning shots.'

Robson's message to his fellow coaches at the UEFA gathering, said Roxburgh, was twofold: 'Keep calm – and always give the other coach a problem. Don't just send on a big striker for another big striker. Change it. Give your opponent things to think about. I've seen Bobby make other triple substitutions that have come off. That's why what José did at Newcastle in the FA Cup was interesting – even though it was probably too big a gamble. I think he gleaned a lot about management from Bobby.'

Robson, asked if the merit of being bold with your substitutions might have been one lesson that was absorbed, replied: 'I hope so. Mind you, I don't think he will ever again, as long as he lives, change all three at half-time when the score is tight. You do that when you're losing 3–0 at half-time and stuffed anyway. The thing to do is change two and hold one in reserve – then maybe stick him on with twenty minutes to go. Yes, I have made triple substitutions. I went to Liverpool a few years ago and sent three on when we were 3–1 down with twenty minutes to go. We drew 3–3. Even twenty minutes from the end it's a gamble. But forty-five minutes is too long, as José discovered. He was a little too bold that day, a little too confident in himself.'

Mind games: the fourth hat?

At the height of the controversy over José Mourinho's reaction to the first-leg defeat Chelsea sustained in Barcelona and the subsequent retirement of the match referee, Anders Frisk, a few people suggested that I obtain a videotape of some of Mourinho's appearances at press conferences and take it to a psychologist. So I consulted a friend of a friend who happens to be a psychoanalyst. He said it would be a waste of time: 'You have to bear in mind that almost every conversation Mourinho has is part of his work, and that the ultimate purpose of each of these communications is not to communicate as such but to increase his team's chances of winning. In a press conference, he is not talking to the people in the room so much as those beyond – his players, other managers, the FA and so on. The advice I would give is the sporting equivalent of what every political interviewer should constantly be asking themselves: "Why is this lying bastard lying to me?"'

Mourinho has couched it in language which would get past the Speaker of the House of Commons. 'Talking to the media is part of the game,' he has said. 'When I go to a press conference before a game, in my mind the game has already started. When I go to a press conference after the game, the game hasn't finished yet. Or, if the game has finished, the next one has already started.' He has also said that both he and Sir Alex Ferguson like these mind games and they certainly seem no more able to resist them than the player who is unable to keep his tugging hands off a passing opponent's shirt. Indeed Mourinho and Ferguson, when opponents in England, appeared as hopelessly addicted to the mind-game habit as storm-bound gamblers betting on which of two raindrops rolling down the outside of a window will be the first to reach the sill. Whichever metaphor you chose, it was the competitive instinct at work. Plus, perhaps, an element of ego in the case of Mourinho, whose maintenance of contact with his homeland through frequent appearances in the Portuguese media could not be explained by the frequently aired theory that the publicity he attracted took pressure off his players.

It was not as if he was consistent. In November 2004, after Wenger had done a Ferguson and ranted at a fourth official during a Champions League match in Eindhoven, a soft-focus Mourinho sought to portray himself as the match officials' friend, saying: 'I feel like an angel when I see how other managers behave in relation to referees and fourth officials. I let these people do their work and get on with mine.' To the protestation that he had been involved in several rows with referees in Portugal, he responded that he had become calmer since moving to England. This struck me as very clever: the kind of thing that, one day down the line, might have earned Chelsea a marginal decision. And rather nice too, a most welcome note of calm sanity amid the turbulence of the English game. A couple of months later, however, Mourinho was insulting Frisk and being escorted down the Cardiff tunnel. Some angel.

The suspicion was that Mourinho simply enjoyed the sound of his voice, especially when it was being mischievous. Few Chelsea players would have disagreed with Deco, who burgeoned under Mourinho at Porto, when he said: 'In the dressing room Mourinho is quite relaxed, but when he gets talking to the press he likes to wind things up – he is playing a role.' But he does know when to stay quiet in his team's interests, unlike the more experienced Ferguson, whose head-to-head record in mind games against Mourinho is unimpressive. When Manchester United went to play Porto, the pair clashed in the technical area, Ferguson angrily complaining to Mourinho (so the fourth official could hear) about his players' perceived exaggeration of the impact of tackles. Ferguson kept up the campaign in the press before the second leg, and one or two United players weighed in with some taunts along the line that their adversaries had been girlish. It was a little unpleasant. Yet, after it had backfired, both Ferguson and Gary Neville were quick to knock on Porto's dressing-room door and wish them all the best in the next round.

Ferguson would be worth a place in any mind-game hall of fame. He might even have helped to define the art with his demand that Leeds United try their damnedest against Newcastle towards the end of the 1995–96 season, when Kevin Keegan's team were being challenged for the title by Ferguson's. Keegan, interviewed by Sky while wearing headphones – never an aid to a middle-aged man's dignity – exuded indignation as he declared how he would 'love it, really love it, if we beat them' and was widely believed to have unsettled his own players at that moment. Although the season was all but over, United had come from a long way behind to take the title and, ever since, the words of the managers have constituted a large proportion, perhaps inordinately so, of the media's coverage of Premier League football. But Ferguson, when he had another chip at Mourinho in the 2004–05 season, again came off second best. He said Chelsea might struggle when they had to travel to the north. True, they had lost at Manchester City – where Keegan was in charge – but once Ferguson's jibe had been brought to their attention they took full points at Everton, Liverpool and Blackburn before clinching the title at Bolton. And then they won at Manchester United when they didn't need to.

Yet he and Ferguson get on well personally. 'I respect Sir Alex,' Mourinho said towards the end of the 2004–05 season, 'but not just respect – I like him. He is a person to fight with but a person who, when the game ends, I can share a glass of wine with and speak openly.' A sign that Ferguson reciprocated those feelings was that he had poked fun at Mourinho through the press, accusing him of offering 'some cheap Portuguese plonk' when United went to Stamford Bridge. Mind games could be seen as hard banter in that neither side wishes to lose face. But every coach to whom you speak insists that they have a serious purpose. 'He wants to protect his players,' said Louis van Gaal. 'I am certain of that. I do it. And I find it logical that a coach should look for a way of helping his team to win the game. You can condition the environment for your players. Maybe he went too far in Barcelona, but later it came out that Frank Rijkaard *had* spoken to the referee, so there was an element of truth in what Mourinho said.'

An element. But surely he was still wrong to accuse Frisk of favouring Barcelona? 'Yes,' said Van Gaal, 'but a lot of coaches have said a referee's decision was wrong and been vindicated by television. I think the referee is always the main influence in a game. Mourinho got emotionally involved, because he is an emotional man – he always was, and now he can show it – and maybe he regrets the business with Frisk, but he cannot rewind the tape and wipe out what happened, so he has to go on. Such are the errors a coach makes at the beginning of his career.' We cannot say with any certainty that Mourinho's Barcelona antics worked for his team in the Champions League, but it is a fact that they eventually ousted Barcelona with a goal that should not have been allowed. As for the questionable goal-line decision that Mourinho claimed went against them at Anfield, it may actually have worked in their favour. That is on the assumption that the referee would otherwise have awarded a penalty and dismissed Petr Čech.

What we could safely assert was that Mourinho would not stop playing these games. They are not prerequisites of footballing achievement; Rafael Benítez did not indulge in them before Liverpool knocked Chelsea out of the Champions League or won the 2005 final. In Istanbul, on the morning after Liverpool had completed one of the most amazing European triumphs by recovering from a 3–0 deficit to beat Milan on penalties, I asked Benítez why he scorned these little ploys. He smiled and replied: 'Maybe my English is not good enough at the moment.' So he had done it in the past, with Valencia? 'No. I prefer to concentrate on working with my team. It is more important.' Nor did Luiz Felipe Scolari, Marcello Lippi or Vicente del Bosque feel the need to play mind games while steering Brazil, Italy and Spain to success in the past three World Cups. They are just part of Mourinho's style and, given what he has won thus far, unlikely to become unfashionable. To quote Desmond

Morris: 'The manager has become a performer and the good manager will always support his team.' So the handsome young twelfth man of Chelsea would toy with the minds of opponents and referees and every other form of authority for as long as they let him get away with it. To the minds of many people, what Mourinho said about Frisk was unacceptably impudent. Yet again some words of Machiavelli are apposite: 'Fortune, like a woman, is friendly to the young, because they show her less respect, they are more daring and command her with audacity.'

PART FIVE

Behind the mask

Humourless?
You're having a laugh

A stranger arriving at Chelsea's training ground between June 2004 and September 2007 might never have guessed that the dark and handsome man in the tracksuit was the boss. Mostly José Mourinho just went about his business deep in thought. Beneath the placid surface, however, was a volatile temper that kept people on their toes. Everyone knew the seriousness with which he took matters of detail, and when he felt that the heads of subordinate departments had not matched it, loud bellowing was often heard from the unfortunate's office. Neil Frazer, the doctor who left a few months after Mourinho's arrival, suffered on several occasions, notably when the wrong X-rays of Arjen Robben were produced. It could happen during matches too. Towards the end of a robust affair at Blackburn, the midfielder Tiago was called off and, when he came to the bench, the staff were not able to provide one of the replenishments required for a substituted player: it might have been a drink, or a tablet. Mourinho exploded and within seconds the physiotherapist, Mike Banks, was sprinting down the tunnel to the dressing room to fetch the missing item.

In consequence, things rarely went wrong and Mourinho's behaviour was polite and charming, if brisk; he hated to waste time. People were told what he wanted and it was done. Very little happened without his being consulted, even if its link with the football side of the operation was tenuous. This was relatively new to him, this broad English view of the job, and, although it led to the odd tense moment with the chief executive, Peter Kenyon, he rather liked it. But he was happiest among the players and, when they came in for training, he joined them as they put their kit on and swapped tales. When they poked merciless fun at the masseur, Billy McCulloch – every dressing room has someone who serves as the butt of jokes – Mourinho joined in the laughter. It would have been hard to imagine Sir Alex Ferguson doing all of that, let alone Arsène Wenger. Or indeed the late Brian Clough. Yet in the early stages of Mourinho's time in England, and especially in the aftermath of Clough's death, a frequent criticism of the newcomer was that he lacked a sense of humour.

Alan Hansen, once the most elegant of defenders with Liverpool and now a *Daily Telegraph* columnist, put it thus after Mourinho had complained that Tottenham had 'parked their bus' (played ultra-defensively) at Stamford

Bridge: 'When Clough talked his mind – and I certainly never agreed with him all the time – he did so with one important quality in evidence. He was funny. Mourinho, for all his colourful opinions, is never funny. And we all know how hard it is to like someone who seems to lack a sense of humour.' I suppose it depends how you define a sense of humour, but, if it involves a readiness to smile, even when the figure of gentle fun is yourself, Mourinho could hardly be found deficient. On the day he was banned from the dugout at Boavista, and Porto won 1–0 under the notional control of his assistant Baltemar Brito, he rang his players at half-time on the speaker-phone that had been smuggled into the dressing room, and told them: 'I'm stuffed. You're beating Boavista 1–0 and Brito is twisting the knife. After the game I'll be unemployed.' The players immediately began chanting, 'Brito is the greatest.' Mourinho clearly relished that for he told the story in his book. He took the joke, too, when Liverpool fans at Stamford Bridge told him to 'Shush' and, the day before, he had been in sparkling form with the press. 'When I arrived here last summer,' he said, stretching his arms wide, 'my ego was this big.' Had it got smaller? He grinned. 'No, it's even bigger!' This brought the house down, but, while his chum Ferguson noted 'a wit and humour about him', a lot of the laughs he coaxed from us were derived from his aura as much as any special comic gift; he got laughs almost as royalty might. When Sir Bobby Robson was told about Hansen's first impression of Mourinho, he replied: 'Well, I can see what he meant. José was sober and serious a lot of the time. But there was plenty of the banter with the players and, as for me, I just thought he was a good lad to be around. I wouldn't like to say he had no sense of humour.' Maybe he just suffered, in this respect, from comparison with Clough, the home-bred iconoclast. As Desmond Morris told me: 'Because Cloughie could be outrageous with a nod and a wink, people weren't as offended as they might have been. He had this northern humour and used it as the sugar coating on the pill of his rudeness.'

But this was only the Mourinho we saw. The person who knows him better than anyone, his wife Matilde – 'Tami', as he calls her – spoke of the mask that often covered his feelings and how she could discern them through a gesture or a look. Mourinho's father was always like that. A friend of the family told me Félix was 'like an electric kettle – on the outside, smooth and steady, but inside boiling'. Mourinho's mother was 'a fighter'. So he had characteristics of both parents. But he was also very much a self-made personality with the knack of being able to separate his private life, such as it had become since he left Portugal, from work. 'I don't like to say that I'm a man with two faces,' he told his audience at the Peres Center in Tel Aviv, 'but José Mourinho the manager and the man are very different. It's important to separate them and I do that very easily.'

The man was seventeen when he found his woman.

She was fourteen. They met at a teenage disco in Setúbal, where Matilde's family had landed after fleeing the newly independent Angola five years earlier; her father had served in the Portuguese forces. Nine years after their meeting, when José was teaching PE and, fortified by the course he had attended in Scotland the previous summer, coaching the Vitória youths, they were wed. Matilde, having graduated from the Catholic University of Lisbon with a degree in philosophy, was soon introduced to the nomadic existence of a football man's wife. First there was the dead-end year with Manuel Fernandes at Estrela da Amadora and then the open road, the times with Robson at Sporting Lisbon, Porto and Barcelona, where the Mourinhos' first child, a girl, was born. They gave her the name Matilde but, in order to avoid confusion, called her 'Tita'. Four years later, their son was born. He got Mourinho's forenames, José Mário, so the infant needed a nickname too and was given 'Zuca'. Until around the time of the Portuguese revolution, it was almost compulsory for parents to hand their first names on to the eldest son and daughter. Today it is seen by many as an irritating anachronism, good for little else than the maintenance of the silly-nickname industry, and remains popular only among aristocratic or conservative families.

José Mourinho is of the latter tradition. Although his goalkeeper father was of relatively humble birth, marriage introduced Félix to the advantages of association with fascist Portugal's ruling class and, given the love and attention that surrounded José as he grew up, he could almost be described as the product of an over-privileged background; at least he did not have to fight his way out of the *favela*, the *barrio* or the ghetto, or leave a remote village at a tender age, like some of those who have acquired fame and fortune through professional sport. But he never asked for an easy ride. The Portuguese, to generalise, are often quite passive people, so much so that in such fields as marketing and the media many key positions in the country came to be occupied by Brazilians; in 2004 the trend even manifested itself in football when Portugal hosted the European Championship and the Brazilian Scolari was in charge of their team. The phenomenon is known as 'reverse colonisation'. It does not affect Mourinho. No territory of his is ever negotiable. Yet he nurses the chip on the shoulder that reminds us of his nationality. No wonder he fitted in so well among those Scots at Largs. Because just as Scotland sometimes feels obscured by England, Portugal lives in the shadow cast by Spain. Or thinks it does.

Mourinho says his friends laugh when he is called arrogant. It does not surprise me because when you walk in his footsteps, you are liable to hear only the opposite. There was the story told by Tosh McKinlay about Mourinho's warm greeting in Glasgow. Not long after I heard this, I happened to be in Lisbon for a UEFA Cup match between Sporting and Newcastle United and met Mourinho's former pupil André Chin, who, having returned to Portugal many years after his family's emigration to Canada, was working at the hotel where I stayed. This was in the spring of 2005. 'I saw Mourinho not so long ago,' he said, 'when he was coach of Porto, around the middle of the season when they won the Champions League. I went to buy some fried chicken in this place near our house in Setúbal and there he was. He looked at me and I recognised him. I held out my hand and asked if he remembered me and then it dawned on him. "André Chin," he said. "How long is it?" I said it had been sixteen or seventeen years. "My God," he said, "that's a long time. What have you been doing?" He always showed an interest in people. We spoke for about fifteen minutes and then he left. He's a great guy and deserves all the success he gets.'

A similar conclusion was reached by Ian Ross, director of communications at Everton Football Club since 2001, former journalist, long-standing friend of mine and, by his own admission, a 'cynical old bastard'. He told me that, in his years at Goodison Park, no one had made more of a personal impact as Mourinho. 'The habit here,' Ross explained, 'is that the visiting manager wanders around the tunnel and dressing-room area, keeping himself to himself and having next to no contact with our staff. There are exceptions – Arsène Wenger, for example, who, if there's a lunchtime game on, comes up and very politely asks if he can watch it on television in the press room. People appreciate his good manners. Mourinho, on his first visit, just shuffled around with his hands in the pockets of his famous overcoat, greeting everyone and saying how welcome he'd been made and how he'd heard a lot about Everton. And I don't just mean executives of the club. I mean he spoke to stewards and ball-boys as well. Sometimes people are in awe of the likes of Mourinho – but he was going up to them! The word spread around the club and, by the time he'd left, there was a sort of euphoric atmosphere around the place, as if it were a shopping mall that David Beckham had just been through. But it wasn't just his charisma. Mourinho had actually taken time out to have a laugh with people and make jokes about our battle with Liverpool for fourth place. He was full of respect for the history of the club, and for David Moyes as a coach. Now I am a cynical old bastard, but I value courtesy above all else and it didn't matter to Mourinho that he was speaking to people who had next to nothing compared with him. He was completely at his ease – and made sure they were. Like Wenger, he always introduced himself by name. He was, quite literally, unassuming. He lit the whole place up.'

Moyes didn't find him arrogant either. 'We had a drink and a chat down at Chelsea,' said the Everton coach, 'and I think the persona he puts over may be for the media. I suspect that behind it he's got the same fear of failure most of us have. It's what probably drives him. At our place, he didn't come in for a drink, funnily enough. He'd come up to me on the bench and shaken my hand when there were still two minutes to play. He'd been criticised a couple of weeks before for not shaking Mark Hughes's hand at Blackburn and I think the gesture to me was his way of saying, "I understand what you do in this country and I respect it. I'm not sure where it fits in my list of priorities. I'm maybe more interested in going to shake my own players' hands than the opposition manager's." I can't be sure. I may be off the mark there. But I think that, when he incurred a lot of the criticism, he was still finding his feet in a new country.'

There could be no more telling testimonial to a Chelsea coach than one from a Fulham supporter. It was at Craven Cottage, Fulham's attractive riverside home, that I was approached by Ian Aitken, who acts as match-day steward in the press room. 'The first time Mourinho came here,' said Aitken, 'we were walking along the touchline from the dressing rooms so he could be taken in to face the press – it's part of my job to escort the visiting manager – when he suddenly looked across the pitch and said he loved the stadium. "Of course you do," I said. "You've just won 4–1." And he said, "No, I've always loved this place – it's so old and traditional." I presumed he knew it through the Bobby Robson connection [Robson both played for and managed Fulham]. Then, when they came back in the Carling Cup, I was expecting him to talk about the game. And he suddenly asked if I'd seen the film *The Incredibles*. I said I hadn't and he told me it was marvellous. For a lifelong Fulham supporter to like the Chelsea manager is unusual, but I found him delightful – charming.'

Sir Bobby Robson recalled Mourinho having an affection for the cinema: 'He'd talk of little but football. Except films. He loved them. I remember him once coming to me and saying, "Mister, I saw a great movie last night. You must go and see it. It was *Forrest Gump*."' A film or meal with his wife is Mourinho's idea of a night out. He seldom drinks. When away, he relaxes by watching films on his laptop or reading. In his first winter in England, asked which book he had on the go, he named the autobiography of the Colombian Nobel Prize-winner Gabriel García Márquez. He reads the occasional novel. His books are usually recommended by Matilde, an insatiable consumer of literature. She also bought his grey cashmere coat, the one which became famous; it came from Armani, cost £1,200 and, at the end of a season during which it came to symbolise Chelsea's success, Mourinho announced that it was to be auctioned in aid of a children's cancer charity with which the club had become associated.

José – or 'Zé Mário', as he is affectionately called – 'Tami', 'Tita' and 'Zuca' lived amid the stuccoed splendour of Eaton Square in Belgravia for their first year in London, before finding a home close to Chelsea's training ground in Surrey. They still cherished their other home in Setúbal, a fine edifice in its own right. Friends say they are unlikely ever to abandon José's roots, the place where he encountered so much pleasure and one particularly tragic episode of pain: he was called back from Barcelona for the death through septicaemia of his sister Teresa, a diabetic who had never recovered from the break-up of her marriage some years before and suffered from a distressing variety of problems. Except to those closest to him, Mourinho never spoke about it: the mask descended. 'I think she was always a worry for him,' said a friend.

Teresa, before her health failed, had been vivacious and extremely pretty. Looks ran in the family and José's have undoubtedly contributed to his success; not just his fame and sex-symbol status but his effectiveness as a coach. 'People in football hardly mention this,' said Desmond Morris, 'but he is an incredibly handsome man, film-star handsome, and it's the combination of that and his behaviour which really works. If he were an ugly little man, his style wouldn't be as effective.' Mainly because players are only too eager to accept him as one of them; they respect him all the more because of his attractiveness to women. It is not so much necessary for any coach as specifically helpful to this one. He is cool. 'If you were to cast someone to play him in a movie,' said Morris, 'it would have to be James Dean.' Indeed; for he is dark and brooding and redolent of youth culture. The youth culture of this or any other age.

Although Mourinho has said his life is a typical

Portuguese combination of the three Fs – Family, Football and Fatima (religion) – and has stressed that he keeps the work in a separate compartment, there does seem to be an element of narcissism about him that makes the limelight-hogging a labour of love. In other words, it must come from within and cannot be explained away by the assertion that a lot of nice actors play villains. But so what? He entertains us and has not hurt too many people. With the notable exception of our old friend Anders Frisk. Even that unalloyed fan Desmond Morris could not talk Mourinho out of this one: 'It was something he very much wanted to hear [the report by two Chelsea staff members that the Barcelona coach had been in the referee's room] and so he adopted it. In the heat of the moment, he made the mistake of saying he had seen it when he hadn't. The whole thing then became a bad smell and he didn't want to know about it.' But then, you may recall, he made his tasteless joke on Portuguese television about being unable to discuss the performance of a Portuguese referee in case he quit: a joke that tended to vindicate those ambivalent towards Mourinho's status as a wit.

So that surge of power that Robson talked about, that licence to insult that distinction in sport affords, had carried Mourinho over the line once or twice. But it did not make him a bad person.

Different class

Now a guessing game. See how many clues you need. Our man is a bright and ambitious coach who came to England in the summer of 2004 having just won European silverware. He joined one of the Premier League's biggest clubs and, upon being introduced to the squad, laid down some principles. He insisted that the players must behave as a unit both on and off the field. They must eat together, for instance, and stay at the table until the last man has finished, in order to prevent the formation of cliques. No player could place himself above the team or act like a star. 'The team,' he declared, 'is the star.' Having followed these instructions, they had a dramatically successful first season under his command. He was Rafael Benítez. But it might have been José Mourinho, because most coaches espouse the same notions, by and large. Few, so far as I am aware, encourage their players to develop laziness, selfish individualism or wilful disobedience.

The differences between Benítez and Mourinho were matters of emphasis or personality and these might be connected with each other. Take their respective attitudes towards mind games: disdain in one case (at least until Sir Alex Ferguson got under his skin in January 2009 and he responded with a list of 'facts'), keen relish in the other. So naturally the past managers with whom Mourinho has been compared are the larger-than-life characters, above all Brian Clough. Yet, according to one of Clough's key players at Nottingham Forest, their ways of going about the job could scarcely be more contrasting. Frank Clark was brought to Nottingham almost as soon as Clough arrived, from Newcastle United, where he had been captain. He was thirty-one and dropping a division and could not even have dreamed he would be a European champion when his career ended in a haze of champagne four years later. But it happened. Forest were promoted in his second season, champions of England the next season and champions of Europe the season after that. They were to retain the European title, too, after Clark had retired and been replaced by Frank Gray. In the league table of footballing fairy tales, then, Clough's Forest will always stand above even Mourinho's Porto.

The decades which separate the careers of Clough and Mourinho are partly responsible for the contrast. 'Mourinho obviously studies the opposition in great detail,' said Clark. 'He spends hour after hour preparing his team for their next opponents, if necessary changing tactics from game to game. Brian hardly considered the opposition. He used just to tell us to play our game, a simple 4–4–2, because that was what we knew best. A lot more thought goes into the game today. But Brian, if he were around now, would probably be sticking to his philosophy.' Yet Clough was utterly unorthodox in other respects. Could you imagine Mourinho ordering the coach driver to pull off the M62 on the way to Liverpool and having him unload crates of beer intended for the post-match celebration? Then inviting his players to have a couple of drinks just a few hours before the kick-off? Yet Clough did that. Forest, 2–0 up from the home leg of their European Champions' Cup first-round tie against the holders, came away with a scoreless draw that night and went on to beat Malmö in the final. 'You had to be something truly special to get away with such ways of managing people,' said Clark, 'and Brian was, quite simply, a genius. There is, though, something of Brian in Mourinho's personality: the total belief in what he's doing and the fact that he's not afraid to voice an opinion.'

Few, since Clough, have made such an astonishing impact on the European game as Mourinho. Within two and a half years of going solo, he had won the UEFA Cup and a year later his Porto were champions of the continent. Clough rose swiftly enough. But he had six years at Derby, where he also won the domestic title and guided his side to the Champions' Cup semi-finals (they lost to Juventus), before working his miracles at

Nottingham. In terms of triumphant entrances to the top-level coaching scene, it is hard to find challengers for Mourinho. One would be Fabio Capello, whose Milan secured the Italian title in each of his first three years and celebrated the hat-trick with a quite magnificent Champions League final victory over Barcelona in 1994. But there are not too many other candidates. Rafael Benítez is one of the few – in four seasons he won the Spanish title twice and the UEFA Cup with Valencia and the Champions League with Liverpool – but at least the Spaniard had an apprenticeship. It remains to be seen whether Mourinho can emulate Capello in maintaining his standard for fifteen years; Capello guided Juventus to the Italian championship in 2005 and 2006 (though both titles were later revoked in the aftermath of a scandal) and then returned to Spain to pick up a second title with Real Madrid before taking over the English national squad at the beginning of 2008. But if Mourinho does pass the test of such a span of time, you can be sure we shall hear plenty about it.

The 250 Israeli and Palestinian coaches who took diligent notes of his ninety-five-minute lecture in Tel Aviv in February 2005 might, however, have been wasting their time, in the sense that only Mourinho could make his methods work as they did: while words such as 'faith' and 'unity' are easy enough to say, they are difficult to translate into medals. Only the special ones can make their players grow.

Few men in English football have observed more than Peter Robinson, who, in over thirty-five years as secretary, chief executive and finally vice-chairman of Liverpool, shared in just about every form of triumph the English and European games had to offer. When Robinson joined the club in 1965, the manager was Bill Shankly, a Scot with cropped hair and a fanatical devotion to his team. 'Bill was probably as close as anyone to Mourinho in style,' Robinson told me, 'and yet he was completely different in one way. He was never boastful about himself. Only about his players. He would never have said *he* was a European champion. He would have said his players were. But Mourinho has the same talent for inspiration. Bill could certainly convince the players they were better than they were. By sheer enthusiasm and presence, he could make them feel superior, even though they knew in their hearts they were not. Intelligent lads like Brian Hall used to speak about it in tones of wonder for years afterwards. They were bewitched. That's probably the best word for it.' When Shankly came to Anfield from Huddersfield in December 1959, Liverpool were languishing in the second division. By the time he retired in 1974, they had won the English title on three occasions, the FA Cup twice and the UEFA Cup – and a platform had been built on which four European Champions' Cups were to be placed by Bob Paisley and Joe Fagan's sides in the space of eight years.

During much of Shankly's success, the captain was

Emlyn Hughes, whom he not so much requested as demanded the board buy from Blackpool. 'I've never known Bill so insistent on having a player,' said Robinson. 'Shankly adored Emlyn and Emlyn adored him and that seemed to be the case with Mourinho and John Terry at Chelsea. The manager's drive was always carried on to the field.' How it was instilled was more difficult to define, but Robinson agreed that a film-star presence was another common factor between Mourinho and Shankly. 'Bill, with his haircut and the way he wore his clothes, did have an air of James Cagney, who was still prominent on the screen in those days,' said Robinson, 'though the respect in which his players held him was mainly due to his knowledge of football and one hundred per cent devotion to it.'

Desmond Morris recalled Shankly: 'He wasn't particularly handsome, but he was charismatic. I met Bob Paisley once at Anfield – and he might have been the chap who looked after the boots. But Shankly had an extraordinary presence. Similar to Mourinho's. If you asked me who would be in the same category as Mourinho, I'd say Shankly and Clough. He has Clough's unpredictability.' Although Clough had a singular way of addressing people – 'he called them "young man", regardless of their age, in order to establish seniority' – Mourinho, too, could hold our attention. 'You hang on his words. He says things which are relevant and thought-provoking. He avoids clichés. He hasn't fallen into the slovenly "at the end of

José points out how many trophies he's won for Chelsea, as he's about to lift the FA Cup after victory over Manchester United (*Press Association*).

Scenes from the final season: a disgruntled Mourinho is distinctly unimpressed at Villa Park (*PA*); more frustration on the touchline during José's final match at Stamford Bridge, against Rosenborg (*PA*); Chelsea fans demonstrate outside Stamford Bridge the morning after the Special One departs (*AFP/Getty Images*).

Scenes of triumph from the semi-final and final of the 2010 Champions League, as Mourinho leads Inter to the trophy in characteristically understated fashion (*both PA*). Marco Materazzi, for one, was devastated upon Mourinho's departure from the San Siro (*Getty Images*).

Mourinho moves
into the Bernabéu,
May 2010 . . . (*PA*).

... the first trophy against Barcelona in the Spanish cup final (*Getty*) ... But Pep Guardiola gets the better of Mourinho over two legs in the Champions League (*PA*).

'I am José Mourinho and I don't change . . .' (*PA*).

the day, that's what it's all about" mentality. He doesn't reach for a hackneyed phrase to get him off the hook. When Mourinho is asked a question, he thinks about the answer. Other managers have made an impression on the country over the years – not just Clough but Tommy Docherty and more recently Alex Ferguson – but I found myself watching all Chelsea matches just because of Mourinho. After one away match, he ordered the players to throw their shirts in the visiting fans' section. He just put a hand on his chest and jiggled his coat – obviously he'd told them to do it in advance and was reminding them. He's always coming up with something new – and surprises are attractive.'

One surprise was his professed adherence to a trait associated with Shankly: in the middle of the 2004–05 season, while Arjen Robben was out of action, Mourinho declared that he gave no thought to injured players. 'I don't want to think about Arjen Robben,' he said. 'I really don't. I think the best way to face an injury to a very important player is to forget him. I don't speak with him. He is in the medical department. When they tell me he is ready to start work with the technical staff, even if he is not a hundred per cent, we shall welcome him with open arms. When my fitness coach says he is ready to play, I will jump for joy. But at the moment I don't want to think about him. I have to support and motivate the others and I would never offer Arjen Robben as an excuse for something. We have the players and we want to work with them.' Shankly operated on the same principles, and although his cold-shouldering of casualties could appear almost heartless – he could hardly look them in the eye – the morale of those available to the cause as their deputies was considered the priority. It was seldom found wanting.

The mind games played with referees or rivals in Shankly's time were never as hard-edged as Mourinho's – and played in private, by and large – while Clough considered referee-baiting or even dissent taboo. 'There were two reasons for this,' said Frank Clark. 'One, Brian thought that was the right way to go about it; and, two, he thought we might get a better response from them if we treated them like human beings.' Trevor Francis, for whom Clough broke the British transfer record in paying Birmingham nearly £1 million in 1979, said: 'The first thing you were told when you came to the club was never to be involved with referees and I think most of the refs around at that time would say we were a pleasure to handle.' Given that they twice brought the European title back to Nottingham, which remains the smallest town ever to receive the honour, it did not appear to do Forest a great deal of harm. Just as Mourinho has his beliefs, so did Clough, and it is too early to compare their efficacy.

Whatever next?

After the 2004–05 season had drawn to a close and the open-topped buses had been returned to their garages, there was a pause to reflect on Chelsea and how far the voyage of discovery might take them. Clearly it would depend on the man at the helm. By whom I mean José Mourinho. The requirement from Roman Abramovich was twofold and quite simple: he had to remain enthusiastic and ridiculously rich. Over the season, Abramovich's enthusiasm had become undeniable (whatever the adventure's purpose, about which he remained silent) and his billions (as estimated by the media) had kept growing. We of modest means were bewildered by this. Did they not have taxation in Russia? Or was Abramovich benefiting from some form of relief for small businesses? It was beyond us. All we understood was that Chelsea would continue to have the biggest player budget in football. Which would entitle them to behave like the biggest club in the world and try to outbid the longer recognised giants from Barcelona, Madrid, Milan and Manchester whenever a major talent became available. This was just the start, Mourinho had trumpeted after Chelsea had won the English championship for the first time in fifty years. So where would it all end?

Back in February 2005, a few days before Chelsea went to Cardiff to collect their first trophy under Mourinho, he told us his new team might not peak until his third season in charge. He might have been buying time – it is something coaches do, as Mourinho has scornfully re-marked, in order to protect themselves from failure – but he explained his timetable fully. Because the gathering of journalists had been called in advance of the trip to Barcelona, he had been asked about the Champions League and, in particular, whether Chelsea at that stage were better equipped for it than his triumphant Porto of the previous season. 'We have better players,' he said, 'but Porto last year were a better team from the tactical point of view – because it was my third year with them. They knew everything I knew! They knew how to adapt just like this [he clicked his fingers]. They could change from system to system. I could start the game with 4–3–3, switch to 4–4–2, change back to 4–3–3. I could press high, put the block low.' But he had been at Chelsea only a matter of months. 'When we get to my third or fourth year, we can say this will be my best Chelsea team. So my contract with Chelsea is the right length.' It had a four-year span then. Now, as well as being more lucrative, it had been extended by a year. Complications in his relationship with Abramovich, however, were to ruin the timetable and upset his plans for the medium term.

Even back in the February of his first season in England, he had been looking forward to a long pre-season in which to prepare for the second. Pre-season is an important time and Mourinho had gone virtually straight from Porto into his first at Chelsea, which had been further affected by comings and goings among the squad in the aftermath of the 2004 European Championship. In February 2005 he was thinking beyond the securing of his first title in England to a proper pre-season, saying, 'I shall be working on things I don't want to work on now. Things must be done in phases and you cannot skip a phase. You have to do one after the other.' He was talking tactics and I asked if they had become more important than individual talent; the issue was topical after the triumphs of Porto and, at the European Championship, Greece. He replied: 'Although it is true that football is becoming more tactical, the fantastic player will always be able to decide a game with a piece of brilliance. And, if you have better players, you can have a better tactical organisation, because they are more intelligent, they understand the game better. It's just a question of whether they want to work for the team. Sometimes big players, if they won't work for the team, fail and smaller players with very good tactical organisation succeed. When you have both, you have the ideal.'

All the indications of his first season were that Mourinho's ability to organise and motivate a team had survived the step up in individual class. Petr Čech, Claude Makelele, Frank Lampard and Arjen Robben were arguably the world's leading players in their positions. John Terry and Damien Duff would have made it to many shortlists. Eidur Gudjohnsen could be said almost to have invented a role for himself; especially in the second half of the season, he had played beautifully. Joe Cole had fulfilled his potential. Yet the roll-call tells its own story. The majority of the squad had already been assembled by the club when Mourinho came. He merely fitted in the Portuguese trio and Didier Drogba (and the athletic Ivorian's hit-and-miss spells were, however temporarily, to place a question mark against Mourinho's judgement). Furthermore, Mourinho had had to hoist Chelsea just one place up the Premier League table to make them champions. But it could not be denied: an improvement of fifteen points since the departure of Claudio Ranieri was conclusive and, if this and the Carling Cup constituted only a start, the mind boggled at the thought of where Chelsea might be when he was finished with them.

In the summer of 2004, when Mourinho boarded Roman Abramovich's yacht for the meeting that was to culminate in his signing of that original contract, he was informed that the intention was to build the world's number-one football club. But Mourinho had created the odd hostage to fortune. Soon after meeting Abramovich he was shown a list that had been prepared for the Russian of top players from around the world and asked which he wanted. He rejected them one by one – the lot. It is reasonable to suppose that the list included Wayne Rooney, and Mourinho explained to the press that Chelsea had declined to challenge Manchester United for the teenager's signature 'because we already have players for that position'. Did he mean Drogba? And the little-used (and later sold to Atlético Madrid) Mateja Kežman? He may, even then, have been beginning to regret one element of this otherwise impressive declaration of independence on footballing matters.

There was no reason to believe, at that stage, that he would seek to leave Chelsea. He told fellow coaches. He told the Portuguese press: 'Nobody can give me a better championship, a better club, a better squad, better players, a better city, a country more passionate for football – nobody can give me a stadium completely full like I have here.' It was a sure sign of the years he spent with Sir Bobby Robson: he was speaking in lists. And the mid-season rumours of his flirtation with the idea of a move to Italy were never truly convincing. When he signed his enhanced contract, after the Champions League semi-final defeat at Liverpool had provided a moment's breather, he said something which, coming from the lips of such an avowed family man, carried far greater resonance than the mid-season hints: 'There is now no doubt that our lives are in London and that is important for my children.'

He was then interviewed on *Match of the Day* after the title-celebration match against Charlton at Stamford Bridge. The opening shot was of Mourinho smiling. The interviewer, Ivan Gaskell, began:

'Chelsea gave you plenty to smile about this season.'

'Yes [Mourinho chuckled], but I'm a special guy, you know ...'

'I've heard that somewhere before ...'

'No, not in that way. Special guy in another way, you know.'

'In what way?'

'I'm not one hundred per cent happy with the season. I'm a bit disappointed. I would like to play in the Champions League final. I was very convinced of that, and people like me, when we don't reach our targets, I think we suffer more than ... people who are happy with a few things.'

'Room for improvement, then?'

'It's not easy to improve a squad of champions, but we can improve a little bit. The supporters will have to try to improve. To support more the team, like some clubs in this country when they play at home.'

'And the press? Improve them too?'

'I think it's impossible to change.'

He did not look like a disappointed man. His smile was not so much broad as deep. It belied the pensiveness of his sentiments. But – and here the words of our psycho-analyst friend of a friend resound – Mourinho was not really trying to communicate with us. He was starting to condition his players for the next season (they seemed to get the message and responded with a superb win at Old Trafford three days later). And he was reminding the supporters that they, too, had been beaten by Liverpool.

Mourinho, according to his old university lecturer Manuel Sérgio, is 'the ultimate post-modern coach' and, while that is almost self-evidently overblown, there could be no argument with the view that the intellectual level of coaching in England had been raised by his presence. But post-modern? The global concept of coaching is not unique to Mourinho by any means, even if he and his staff have interpreted it brilliantly. He was not the first to play mind games, even if he was such a master of the dark arts that the Chelsea team went through the Barcelona and Bayern Munich episodes believing UEFA were victimising them, and the opposition players – Barcelona's at any rate – being disrespectful. 'He really did create a siege mentality,' one player told me. But no; that could have been Ferguson. I tended to the view that Mourinho had not so much taken the coach's role on to a new level as put an exceptional amount of work into it. Even some of his best friends would concede that his outstanding qualities (the extraordinary charisma apart) were organisation and mental effort. 'Post-modern?' smiled one. 'You must remember that Manuel Sérgio is a philosopher.'

We had observed how Mourinho went about the job. We had learned how this extraordinary coach was formed. What we did not know is how long his success would endure. And where he would go once the Chelsea project matured. At that stage it was tempting to believe that he would go nowhere. After all, his great rivals Ferguson and Wenger were long-serving managers. On the other hand, it was hard to see Mourinho as the dynastic type. The only hints at to what his future might hold were that Italian hankering and a more firm ambition to lead the national team of the country of his birth. He told Andy Roxburgh: 'I would not like to retire without having been coach of Portugal.' And explained to the Portuguese newspaper *A Bola*: 'I want to do something that is for everybody. I want to help them be, one day, a little bit happier.' He spoke of how important a single international appearance had been for his father and added: 'My career as a coach will only make sense when, in a few years, I have the opportunity to train the national squad.'

During his visit to Tel Aviv in March 2005, he put a rough timescale on it. 'I want to work for another thirteen years,' he said, 'and one thing is compulsory to me. I want to be manager of Portugal – when I want it. I want to manage my country for maybe two or four years, at a World Cup or European Championship. That leaves eleven or nine years in my career and I see myself staying in English football until then.' Unless, he added after the season had finished, an opportunity arose to try a club in Italy at some stage (that bit was to come true when he joined Internazionale). But the resolve to lead Portugal's national team remained fundamental.

What, though, would Mourinho be doing after all that, when, at the age of fifty-five, having stepped down as Portugal's coach following their success in the 2018 World Cup – perhaps the trophy would have been lifted by their ageing captain, Cristiano Ronaldo, once of Manchester United and Real Madrid – he retires? Would he be content to sit reading on one of the beaches near Setúbal? Maybe for a month or two. But my guess is that, long in advance, he would have explored other avenues. Broader avenues than football could provide.

While the Barcelona controversy was raging, Mourinho – as if to demonstrate that there was no such thing as bad publicity – became the new face of American Express in Europe and Asia. 'Why Asia?' he asked the people from the credit-card company, who told him he was as much an icon there as in Europe. He found that interesting and the trip to Israel, too, appeared to capture his imagination. 'When I have retired,' he said in Tel Aviv, 'when, in thirteen more years, I have finished with football, I can see myself one hundred per cent involved in human actions. I have always thought about problems in the Middle East and Africa, not just about football.' He had often denied any interest in politics, by which we could presume he meant party politics, but there would surely be something to suit his talents at the United Nations. He had, after all, proved he could unite dressing rooms. But this was for the future too and many a football man had toyed with ideas of harnessing his power only to have second thoughts when the tiresome details of life in the slow lane become evident.

Mourinho went off for his 2005 summer holidays – the family made a beeline for Setúbal – around the time that England celebrated the eightieth wedding anniversary of Percy and Florence Arrowsmith, who were said to be the world's longest-married couple. Asked for any advice she could give people anxious to emulate the success of her relationship with Percy, the senior partner at 105, Florence, aged 100, replied: 'Never be afraid to say sorry.' Meanwhile Anders Frisk, a fugitive from a murkier world than the Arrowsmiths', was in Sweden watching his daughter ride her horse and his sons play football in the time his duties for an insurance company left free. A Champions League referee only four months earlier, his heart set on a career climax at the 2006 World Cup (for which he had already been invited by FIFA to train), Frisk now had no official involvement in football bar the education of young referees. Privately, declining countless interview requests, he awaited some sign of regret from Mourinho for the consequences, however unintended, of the Chelsea coach's questioning of his integrity in the Camp Nou. Mourinho's life had, of course, changed too. 'Especially my family life,' he had said. And I wondered how the Mourinhos would spend the days leading to their second festive season in London. Maybe José and Matilde would take their two children ice-skating in the little square off the King's Road and be like any other happy family, their eyes shining under the Christmas lights and oblivious to the darkness beyond.

The mixture as before

The selective myopia of José Mourinho continued through his second successful year as Chelsea coach. As he and his family celebrated their second Christmas in England – there was no skating off the King's Road now, for they had moved to Surrey – his team were in their familiar place at the top of the Premier League. Nor were Chelsea seriously challenged. They had won each of their first nine matches and, although the concession of two points at Everton had been followed by a 1–0 defeat at Manchester United, few observers harboured the slightest doubt that Mourinho would again end the English season with a magnum of champagne in his hands. Yet this time, for all that Chelsea secured the title in the most satisfactory manner with a resounding 3–0 victory over Sir Alex Ferguson's United at Stamford Bridge, there was to be a sour taste on his lips.

In an extraordinary press conference after the match,

Mourinho began by saying how nice it was for the team to have become champions again in front of the mass of their own supporters rather than only the diehard travellers who had obtained tickets for Bolton a year earlier. He even pleased and amused the journalists with his explanation of why, having been presented with his medal on the pitch, he hurled it – along with his jacket – into the crowd in the Matthew Harding Stand: 'I think the people behind that goal are the best supporters we have. One of the reasons we are champions is that we have a good record at home and they are a part of that, so I wanted to share the moment with them. The person who got the medal is a lucky guy. He has a great souvenir.' Mourinho paused briefly and, smiling, added: 'Or he can go on eBay and make a fortune!' No sooner had the laughter subsided than Mourinho was changing mood. Using a glass of water on the table in front of him to illustrate a brief lecture on economics, he declared: 'In this country, where people see only coins and pounds and transfer fees, this is the worst club to be a manager. Because to win is never enough.' And then he got to the nub of his discontent. 'I won nine consecutive matches at the start of the Premier League season and, after that, I won a lot of other matches. Yet I was never Manager of the Month. Not once!' Because of the lack of appreciation this signified, Mourinho implied, he had considered quitting a couple of times during the season. Having let this unexpected shower fall on Chelsea's parade, he was off – with barely a mention of any of the players who had made club history (though he did generously express a hope that Wayne Rooney, who had fractured a foot during the match, would recover in time for the forthcoming World Cup in Germany).

At first it did strike us as odd that he had not picked up at least one or two of the monthly awards, which are made by the Premier League's sponsors, Barclays, after due consideration by a panel of several dozen representatives of sections of the game including managers, supporters, television and radio commentators and journalists, of whom I am one. But then I thought back to the voting process. At the end of the first month of the season, for example, the main candidates were Mourinho and Paul Jewell of Wigan Athletic, whose team had just been promoted yet were playing splendidly (even Mourinho had sportingly admitted they were unlucky to lose to Chelsea on the opening day). The race was close, but some of us took into account the disparity in background and resources between Wigan and Chelsea: after all, we reasoned, if the award were given on the basis of results alone, a computer could do it, making our deliberations redundant.

When I mentioned this the following day on the Sky television programme *Jimmy Hill's Sunday Supplement*, my colleague Brian Woolnough of the *Daily Star* disclosed that he had instigated a forceful post-match exchange of words at Stamford Bridge with Simon Greenberg, the director of communications, who had loyally defended Mourinho from the accusation that, in appearing to elevate his own petty peevishness over the achievements of his players, he had done the club a disservice – and not for the first time. I thought Woolnough's point a good one. By now, surely, the familiar argument that Mourinho's moans and groans and outrageous allegations were no more than a diversionary tactic calculated to take the pressure off his players had been discredited; what pressure could the players possibly have been under once the last title available to them in the season, the Premier League, had been won? Chelsea may have fallen short in the Champions League, losing in the first knockout round to Barcelona, who avenged their defeat the previous season on merit despite Mourinho's risible claims that a theatrical fall by the brilliant teenager Lionel Messi had caused the dismissal of Asier del Horno at the Bridge. They may have paid for Mourinho's employment of a strange formation in the FA Cup semi-final against Liverpool by missing out on an opportunity of the domestic double. But in the Premier League they had once again been the best, leaving no room for argument.

In the build-up to United's visit, Sir Alex Ferguson had been making much of his team's late surge and growling that Chelsea could expect more of a struggle for the title in the next campaign. And he was to be proved right there. The response from Mourinho's players on this occasion, however, was a majestic triumph, rounded off with glorious goals from Joe Cole and Ricardo Carvalho. So much, they seemed to be saying, for the closing of the gap. Chelsea lost their two remaining matches – characteristically, Mourinho complained about the referees having one law for Chelsea and one for the rest – but it was time to salute their consistency. All season they had dropped a mere two points at home; indeed they had never lost at home in the Premier League in two years under Mourinho (whose personal run was only just beginning). They were a team of unrivalled efficiency. So, after half a century without a championship, Chelsea had two in a row.

'Consecutive' – that is how Mourinho described his titles as he savoured them. Consecutive. He had this new word of which he made all the more proud use because he, personally, had four in a row, if you included the pair he had picked up in Portugal – which he made sure you did. The efficacy of his methods had survived the improvement in United's performances and rumoured discontent among the players. I did not take the latter too seriously; it was inevitable that some players would be unhappy when left out.

To give Mourinho his due, he did not appear to favour his own buys in matters of team selection. Among those to suffer were Del Horno and one of the more expensive purchases, Shaun Wright-Phillips, although the midfielder Michael Essien, to whom Mourinho had switched in the summer of 2005 after Steven Gerrard had finally, at the eleventh hour, decided to stay at Liverpool, settled into English football quickly (even if, more than once, his tackling raised eyebrows and hackles). Mourinho also kept faith in Drogba. A sometimes surly fellow, unpopular even with many Chelsea supporters due to his propensity for falling to the ground and staying there, he was widely pilloried in the media, but proved his worth towards the end of the season and went on to explore the boundaries of greatness. Wright-Phillips, whom Sven-Göran Eriksson left out of England's World Cup squad, went off for his holidays perhaps wishing he had stayed at Manchester City, or at least left them for Arsenal rather than Chelsea. Tiago, meanwhile, had been obliged to move to Essien's erstwhile club at Lyon in order to revive his career – under Gérard Houllier, France's outstanding club not only retained their domestic title but reached the Champions League quarter-finals – and his compatriot Maniche, having rejoined Mourinho in mid-season, hardly became the toast of all London.

So Mourinho completed his second year supreme in terms of winning Premier League matches but with a dubious record in the transfer market: certainly not one to compare with Sir Alex Ferguson at his peak, let alone Arsène Wenger.

Mourinho's principal talents clearly lay in other directions. Tactically, for instance, his countless triumphs outweighed the occasional disaster and Chelsea's ninth victory of that opening burst was a classic. Having let Bolton take the lead through Stelios at the Bridge, they went in for the interval to discover that Mourinho had devised an enterprising substitution. Off went the left-back, Del Horno, on went an extra attacker, Eidur Gudjohnsen, and a 3–3–4 formation produced four goals in the space of nine minutes – two each from Drogba and Frank Lampard – before Gudjohnsen rounded off a 5–1 triumph. Crisis? What crisis? True, an eventful spell had also featured the dismissal for handball of the visiting defender Ricardo Gardner, but tactical boldness had been rewarded and afterwards Bolton's manager, Sam Allardyce, gave credit where it was due. 'José Mourinho is a major, major asset for Chelsea,' he opined. 'For however long he is here, they can stay at the top and match Manchester United's dominance.' At West Ham a couple of months later, Chelsea were drawing when Mourinho sent on Hernan Crespo, who scored within a minute. There were plenty of other cases of substitutes scoring for Chelsea. When a club's bench regularly contains talent with a total value exceeding £50 million, it is bound to help. But, as always with Mourinho, you had to remember Porto, where his use of less exalted substitutes was already highly skilled. After the defeat at Manchester United, where Darren Fletcher's looping header earned the then maligned Scottish midfield player a brief bask in the warmth of hero-worship, Chelsea went three months without losing. And then, suddenly, they were beaten 3–0 at Middlesbrough, a strange team capable of routing the best in England (United and Arsenal also fell on Teesside) and reaching the UEFA Cup final but not, apparently, of finishing in the top half of the Premier League.

At the end of the season, having taken fourteenth place, Middlesbrough bade farewell to their manager, Steve McClaren, who succeeded Eriksson as England coach. The Football Association took more than three months to make up their minds on the succession. You might have thought that, even if they were unsure about McClaren's part-time work by Eriksson's side over the previous five years, the outwitting of Mourinho, Wenger and Ferguson in the same season would have swung them over more quickly. But then it is not always just the coach who affects the fortunes of a team and, in this context, Chelsea provide a good illustration in the case of Mourinho's captain, John Terry.

Once again, he had exerted a massive influence on the season. The Middlesbrough shock was followed by defeats at home to Barcelona and away – albeit not far away – at Fulham. Three losses in eight matches: by Chelsea's standards, that nearly did add up to a crisis. Their lead in the Premier League had been cut from seventeen points to seven and on 9 April, Palm Sunday – the day Mourinho had erroneously forecast they might make sure of the title – they had West Ham again, at the Bridge. They lost a goal – to James Collins – and then a man, when Maniche was sent off. Yet Chelsea hit back with four goals – from Drogba, Crespo, Terry and Gallas

– and in the *Daily Telegraph* the next day Alan Hansen praised Terry's performance as the perfect answer to those rumours about the dressing room. 'Whenever things were going badly for me as Liverpool captain,' he candidly recalled, 'I wanted to get off the pitch as soon as possible. You could never call me a great captain. But Terry is a great captain. He has obviously said to himself, "Let's get this sorted", and yesterday he was a giant among men. Normally, if the captain is a centre-back, you would expect him to display either battling qualities or composure. Terry possesses both of those qualities in abundance.' He was the kind of inspirational figure towards whom a team could look in times of adversity. And from that moment United knew their pursuit of the champions would be in vain.

By now Chelsea's thoughts of the Champions League were focused on the next season, for which they envisaged introducing three players, including Germany's outstanding midfielder, Michael Ballack, who had so troubled them in the 2005 quarter-final against Bayern Munich, and the devastating Ukrainian striker Andriy Shevchenko from Milan. They had departed the Champions League early in 2006 at the hands of Barcelona, with whom Mourinho clearly still had a problem. When Barcelona returned to the scene of the tunnel fracas the previous year, they exhibited the dignity you would expect from a Rijkaard team as well as the divine technique exemplified by Ronaldinho. On this occasion, however, the dominant character was the slight but abundantly gifted young Messi, whose torment of Del Horno ended when the left-back, after more than one botched attempt (plus an ugly intervention by Arjen Robben), chopped him down and was sent off. Own goals by Thiago Motta and John Terry having cancelled each other out, Samuel Eto'o secured a first-leg lead for Barcelona and most neutrals reckoned they were full value for it. Not Mourinho, of course. He tried to couch his criticism of Messi in humour, observing that Barcelona was a city of culture, with many fine theatres, where he must have gleaned the histrionic arts that had enabled him to roll upon impact with Del Horno, convincing the Norwegian referee Terje Hauge that he had been hurt. But when you stripped away the sarcasm, Mourinho was calling Messi a cheat. Even more gravely in view of the Frisk episode, he was implying that those in charge of matches involving Barcelona could not be trusted to show impartiality.

This, for many of us, was too much to take. But how could we blame Mourinho alone when UEFA let him get away with it? All those fine words after Frisk's premature retirement and the two-match ban imposed on the Chelsea coach – 'We will sanction anyone,' said the chief executive, Lars Christer Olsson, 'who makes inflammatory statements that could jeopardise the security of match officials and bring the game into disrepute' – meant next to nothing because Mourinho's fresh outburst was ignored. Chelsea were even able to pull off a minor propaganda coup on their coach's behalf when they claimed that Del Horno's offence, for which UEFA had disclosed he would be suspended for one match (the customary maximum for a red card is three), had thereby been deemed minor. In fact the punishment seemed no more than fitting for a crime less unsavoury than that of another Chelsea player, Michael Essien, at the group stage; the Ghanaian had made a dangerous lunge at Liverpool's Didi Hamann. Essien was banned for two matches after television coverage of the challenge and Mourinho, when the Sky team next visited Stamford Bridge, sneered at their reporters: 'They are pleased with you in Barcelona.'

Although Mourinho was to prove incapable of inspiring his team to another triumph over the great Catalan club, he was certainly bringing the best out of the media and Her Majesty's press were in especially good form between the two legs of the Barcelona tie, for there is nothing they like better than to dip their bread in the rich gravy of a fall from grace. The *Sunday People*'s trenchant Paul McCarthy accused Mourinho of uttering 'weasel words' and went into well-argued detail: 'What Mourinho said in the aftermath of the Barcelona defeat at Stamford Bridge has a direct link to those morons whose knee-jerk reaction is to threaten somebody's life on the internet. The Chelsea manager's default setting is conspiracy. It's an attitude which panders to the lowest common denominator and those fanatics who believe everything – life, society and football – is against them and that the only response is to kick back against anybody who tries to grind them down. They pick up their cues from their leader, Mourinho, and react in the only way they see fit – by threatening the life of Norwegian referee Terje Hauge.' In fairness to Chelsea, McCarthy added, they had removed such items from their website as swiftly as possible. But was there no one at the club who could tell Mourinho that too often he went beyond the pale? 'All you see is Mourinho surrounded by fawning lackeys who don't have the courage to stand up to him and tell him he's wrong. There is a tainted and twisted view from within the club. They have never lost a big game, they've always been cheated. It's never Chelsea's fault, it's always devious opponents. Or bent referees. Or the scumbag media. It is an ugly, unseemly way to run a football club and that is why I received so many calls from neutrals this week delighted Arsenal had won in Madrid and equally delighted Chelsea had lost to Barcelona.'

In the *Sun*, Steven Howard analysed Mourinho's own altering image: 'The public perception of a man originally greeted as a breath of almost intoxicating fresh air has now deteriorated to a point where he appears to be leaking poisonous gases. Once he was applauded for the winks, nudges and wisecracks because he did it with great style. Now, though, the undoubted charm is wearing thin. No longer viewed as the articulate, well-travelled raconteur complete with amusing riposte to anyone who might ruffle his prolific plumage, he is seen as fantasist, hypocrite and defender of the indefensible. Though blinded by double standards himself, he attempts to pull the wool over others' eyes. In the programme for the first leg with Barcelona, he wrote: "Since our two great teams were drawn together, there have passed weeks in which Chelsea Football Club has said not a single word about this tie. But from Barcelona we have heard revenge, pitch [Chelsea had been accused of delaying the replacement of a worn Stamford Bridge pitch in order that Barcelona would be denied the benefit of the improved surface], battle, revenge, pitch, battle, revenge, pitch, battle." And there, in one daft sentence, Mourinho successfully stuck his thumb in the festering wound.' He was fooling no one. Nor would the press and public, Howard continued, continue to swallow such notions as that of Messi being an actor when they could see that Del Horno, more than his victim, had been feigning injury after the collision, 'in an attempt to evade punishment'. But what could we expect, Howard concluded, from the man responsible for the Anders Frisk affair?

As withering an attack as any – a detailed and scornful description of how the Special One had become the Specious One – came from Hugh McIlvanney in the *Sunday Times*. 'With the wearing banality of muzak,' he wrote, 'the complaints and conspiracy theories of José Mourinho thrum in our ears every time the realities of football deviate from what he sees as the irresistible destiny of his talents. Whether his consistently one-eyed view of events is the result of a genuine taint of paranoia or of calculated use of misinterpretation as a weapon, the effects are bound to be equally tiresome. Hypocrisy is a creature that no amount of meretricious dressing-up can make attractive. As Mourinho repeatedly excuses, tacitly or volubly, egregious offences by his players while un-leashing a torrent of condemnation on the (often lesser) transgressions of others, as he twists facts mercilessly to suggest that rare unfavourable scorelines for Chelsea aren't actually defeats, only injustices, his arguments are laughably self-serving. In his reaction to Barcelona's Champions League victory at Stamford Bridge, a win marred by controversy but certainly not undeserved, he demonstrated yet again that he has become the Specious One. And he is in danger of becoming something worse: a graceless bore. Whereas once his mischief came across as the sophisticated games-playing of a cunning, worldly *provocateur*, amusing us with observations marinaded in irony and jokes tipped with venom that did no more than sting, steadily his methods of seeking to undermine any-body he perceives as an obstacle to his ambitions have coarsened into unacceptable offensiveness. His efforts to portray himself and his team as righteous purveyors of excellence, assailed from all sides by envy, cynicism and devious plots, sometimes relate so strangely to his own manipulative ways that they teeter on the edge of farce.'

*

Why had Mourinho become less popular in the country at large, as reflected by these columnists? His behaviour had certainly become more strident and repetitive and this may have been influenced by the growing tension behind the scenes at Stamford Bridge (though not on the stadium's steep slopes, where Mourinho was greatly loved still, indeed already assured of undying affection). It is unlikely that he was affected by the condemnations of McCarthy, Howard or even McIlvanney.

He hardly appeared a chastened character when his team were knocked out of the Champions League. They enjoyed the better of a low-key first half at the Camp Nou, but Barcelona could afford to be patient because they were ahead on aggregate and in the seventy-eighth minute all doubt as to the outcome was swept away, quite magnificently, by Ronaldinho, who ran straight at the Chelsea defence and, shrugging off Terry as if one of the world's most formidable centre-backs were an irksome child, beat Petr Čech. A few seconds from the final whistle, Frank Lampard equalised on the night with a penalty that had been awarded to Terry by Markus Merk even though Barcelona's Mark van Bommel just got a foot to the ball before Terry's fall. Barcelona did not protest unduly; television replays are a luxury unavailable to referees and the decision had been both marginal and academic. Mourinho, as ever, was discerning only what he wanted to put to use and afterwards, in the press conference, he insisted the 1–1 score had proved that

Barcelona, although they had prevailed on aggregate, had been unable to beat an eleven-man Chelsea: 'For me, the result at Stamford Bridge was crucial.' He did not, of course, mention the dubious nature of the penalty that had preserved his weedy argument. Meanwhile, just off stage in the lecture theatre where he spoke lurked several of his assistants: Rui Faria, Silvino Louro, André Villas-Boas (presumably the others were keeping an eye on the referee's room). It was an unusual scene. Were they there as minders? Or comfort blankets? Either way, it was hard to think of a precedent. Indeed it was impossible to think of a single major European coach who had not been happy to conduct his press conferences alone. What was it Paul McCarthy had written a few days earlier about 'fawning lackeys'? These, to be fair, were worthy football men. But would they have the courage to tell Mourinho when he was wrong?

He seemed to have worked out that something was wrong by the beginning of April, when he was much more his old self in reacting to Manchester United's closing of the points deficit at the top of the Premier League as if it were water and he a duck's back. In fact, feathers and webbed feet were involved in the metaphor on which he artfully alighted as the media gathered to gauge his nerve in the build-up to West Ham's visit to Stamford Bridge. A couple of days earlier, the country's consternation about a long-feared epidemic of the so-called bird flu had grown when a dead swan was noticed in a picturesque Scottish bay. There was, it later transpired, no need for panic, but the results of tests on the swan had yet to be announced and Mourinho, when a reporter asked if he was worried about United's increasing proximity, replied deadpan: 'For me, pressure is bird flu. I am feeling a lot of pressure with the swan in Scotland. I am serious. I am more scared of bird flu than football. What is football compared with life? A swan with bird flu – for me, that is the pressure of the past two days. I have to buy some masks – maybe for my team as well.' It was brilliant, flawless. Not only did he address any psychological doubts his players may have been encountering; he made the rest of us seem shallow, heartless even, for appearing to place the order of football teams above the health of the nation in our list of priorities. The final line was a clever touch, too: family over football. More classic Mourinho. Then there was the Devon Loch nonsense to deal with: the citing by Ferguson and some columnists of the racehorse that, infamously, had fallen when within forty yards of the winning post in the Grand National half a century earlier. 'I know the story,' said a well-briefed Mourinho. 'But I tell you a Portuguese story, because in Portugal there are no Devon Lochs and no horses. We're in the sea, in a boat one mile from the beach. I jump, because I'm a good swimmer. And this fellow wants to race me to the beach. I go, using lots of different swimming styles, and get to the beach, and walk on the beach. When he reaches the beach, he dies. We call it "dying on the beach". He shouldn't chase me! He should say to the boat, "Take me a little bit closer." He's so enthusiastic chasing me, but he has a heart attack. That's our Devon Loch.' A shade brutal in its impact, perhaps, but, as parables go, not the hardest to interpret. And one whose message his team were only too capable of driving home in their next match, with that wonderful recovery from the dismissal of Maniche. And duly, some three weeks later, United swam into West London, their campaign finally to die on the beach.

The celebrations were a little less euphoric than the year before – certainly on Mourinho's part – and the body language between him and his players a little less eloquent. But the pooh-poohing of suggestions that he and Roman Abramovich's project to bestride football would diverge was firm. Ballack arrived, with Shevchenko promising to follow. Mourinho still found time to talk about himself, even if he was doing no more than answer the questions of Henry Winter when he told the *Daily Telegraph* football correspondent: 'When people say negative things about me, my family know what they have at home. They, and other people who know me well, think that sometimes I shouldn't be such a "club man". They say to me, "A lot of managers think more about themselves than the club." With me, I put the interests of the club above my image. That makes my life a little more difficult.' But he added: 'I cannot change. I am the leader of the group. Today it is Chelsea, before it was Porto and tomorrow it could be somebody else. I cannot worry about my own image. Critics cannot change me. No chance! I never hide when my team lose. I can disappear when my team win.' Like he did when they won the title at the Bridge?

The more successful a man becomes in football, the more lackeys he acquires, and the more they fawn, the less he has to make sense; Sir Bobby Robson alluded to it when he spoke of power. It can frequently be found in the anatomy of a winner and in May 2006, after the Barclays panel had met for the last time before dispersing for a World Cup summer, Mourinho was declared Manager of the Year. Not of the month. Of the year. Although he could not attend the presentation dinner, he did send a recording which expressed his gratitude, coupled with a puckish bewilderment about the lack of monthly awards. How, though, could the panel have overlooked his achievement over the year? How could they not acknowledge that although a little of the magic might have worn off, although the love affair with the English people had temporarily faded and Chelsea had become as unpopular as Manchester United, he was still a bit special?

PART SIX

From infighting to ecstasy

A Bridge too far

José Mourinho's last complete season at Stamford Bridge was routine – but only to the extent that it began with a home win and ended with John Terry brandishing a trophy, Chelsea's second of the campaign. It began late in the World Cup summer of 2006 with a triumph over Manchester City in which goals from John Terry, Frank Lampard and Didier Drogba went unanswered and, after two from Drogba had won a stormy Carling Cup final against Arsenal at the Millennium Stadium, ended with Drogba confounding Manchester United in the first FA Cup final at Wembley since the demolition of the original arena in 2000. New stadium; newly familiar hands on the champagne.

On the face of things, little about Chelsea had changed. But the face of things was deceptive. Already there had been persistent rumours of conflict behind the scenes involving Mourinho. The assumption nevertheless was that two English championships in succession guaranteed him omnipotence, at least in matters relating directly to the team, much as Sir Alex Ferguson had earned the right to enjoy at Manchester United. We were to learn otherwise. Nor, given the regularity with which Mourinho had deposited trophies in Roman Abramovich's lap – albeit not the increasingly coveted Champions League – did many observers credit the full disruptive significance of the pre-season dealings. These saw some notable performers from the World Cup arrive at the Bridge: Michael Ballack, vastly experienced leader of the German hosts, came on a free transfer and big wages; Khalid Boulahrouz, a hard man for Holland, was recruited along with Salomon Kalou, an Ivorian teammate of Drogba's and – most dramatically, and most damagingly to Mourinho's professional relationship with Roman Abramovich – Andriy Shevchenko, the great but ageing Ukrainian striker for whom Milan, because they knew a crucial half-metre of pace had left his legs, were happy to take £30 million. Ashley Cole, England's left-back, was to prove the odd man out: an unqualified success. Out went Hernán Crespo, this time for good; William Gallas, to Arsenal in part-exchange for Cole; Eidur Gudjohnsen; Asier De Horno; Robert Huth; Glen Johnson; and Carlton Cole.

While the doorkeepers at the Cobham training ground were getting dizzy as faces came and went, many miles to the north a more tranquil scene could be observed.

The only newcomer at Manchester United's training ground on Carrington Moor was Michael Carrick. Sir Alex Ferguson's squad, into which such key players as Wayne Rooney and Cristiano Ronaldo had already been bedded, was to encounter the minimum of disruption and this was one factor in the transfer of the English title back from Chelsea to United.

There were others. High among them in order of importance were the cracks that had appeared in Chelsea's unity and were to keep widening until Mourinho left the club. Indeed some considered internal politics the crucial reason why Chelsea had relinquished the dominance established in Mourinho's first season, the campaign that had culminated in the 3–1 triumph Old Trafford could not stomach. Only in that season had the politics seemed not to matter. At its end, however, an appointment suggested to Abramovich by Piet de Visser, the veteran Dutch coach and scout on whose advice the owner had come to rely, began to split the club into factions. One group featured Mourinho and his assistants: you might, with due deference to the Scottishness of Steve Clarke and Baltemar Brito's Brazilian origin, have called it the Portuguese faction. The other was created by the arrival of Frank Arnesen as director of football. Although, in his playing days, Arnesen had represented Denmark with distinction, he had spent much of his career in Holland, remaining there for a prolonged and highly successful stint as director of football with PSV Eindhoven before moving to England to join Tottenham Hotspur in the same capacity. At De Visser's instigation, Arnesen had been invited to a close-season meeting on one of Abramovich's yachts and engaged by Chelsea, even though it would entail the payment of compensation to Tottenham of an estimated £8 million. This created the 'Dutch' faction.

Tension soon arose. Mourinho had opposed the appointment of Arnesen, even though the affable Dane had been linked with the emergence at PSV of such stars as Arjen Robben – by now at Chelsea through the De Visser influence and proud possessor of his first Premier League medal – Ruud van Nistelrooy, Jaap Stam and Ronaldo, the great Brazilian. And a year later, when Arnesen and De Visser proposed bringing into the squad Alex, the young Brazilian central defender whom Chelsea had signed from Santos on De Visser's advice but loaned to PSV, Mourinho put his foot down and demanded Boulahrouz instead. He argued, reasonably, that although Hamburg would have to be paid £8.5 million for him, Boulahrouz offered versatility; he could challenge not only John Terry and Ricardo Carvalho in central defence but the likes of Paulo Ferreira and Ashley Cole at full-back. But Boulahrouz was to have difficulties with form and fitness and, after an unsuccessful loan to Sevilla, was sold to Stuttgart at a loss of £4.25 million. Alex, meanwhile, continued to flourish in Holland before being called to Stamford Bridge at the start of the 2007–08 season, shortly before Mourinho's departure, and establishing himself as a worthy successor to Ricardo Carvalho alongside John Terry.

This is not to contend that Mourinho's judgement of a player was inferior to that of Arnesen or De Visser, or vice versa – merely to imply that the tension was not always creative. Mourinho could play office politics as enthusiastically as anyone and had a typically Portuguese defensiveness about his right to manage and control recruitment to the squad as he saw fit. He correctly believed that it was the traditional way in English football. He had, after all, spent many hours discussing it with Sir Bobby Robson and had studied Ferguson with his almost obsessive attitude to control. At Chelsea, the factions never worked together as at Ferguson's United. Instead of a brains trust under the unquestioned command of one executive, Chelsea were run by rivalry, each seeking the favour of the owner. And the factions were at a distance throughout that 2006–07 season. With Mourinho continuing to provoke controversy.

In his first season, he had reacted to a storm of UEFA-led opprobrium over the Anders Frisk affair by accusing the club of not supporting him enough and Abramovich had taken his side, throwing in a substantial pay rise. But, while domestic supremacy was maintained in Mourinho's second season, the big prize from Abramovich's point of view, the Champions League, remained elusive. The question of whether Mourinho was still worth the turbulence that surrounded him must have entered Abramovich's mind, notably when Mourinho made no secret of his disdain for the signing of Shevchenko, upon whose recruitment the owner had personally insisted.

And so the third season of Mourinho began. The eighth League match was to prove one of the most controversial. It was at Reading, where Chelsea won 1–0 despite having two goalkeepers carried off on stretchers. Petr Čech's was the more serious injury: a skull fracture suffered when Stephen Hunt caught him with a knee. A furious Mourinho blamed Hunt and felt so emotional about it three days later, on the eve of a Champions League match against Barcelona, that he not only repeated his accusation against the Reading player but said he wished he could have used stronger language. Mourinho also bitterly criticised Reading FC and the local ambulance service. He claimed that Čech, who was to be out of action for three months and would have to use protective headwear during matches for the rest of his career, could have died because of delays in treatment. He said thirty minutes had elapsed between the Chelsea doctor's call for an ambulance and Čech's departure for hospital. Reading, in turn, deemed Mourinho guilty of 'very serious factual inaccuracies', saying that it had taken just twenty-six minutes between the call for the ambulance and Čech's arrival in – not departure for – hospital. The ambulance service also contradicted Mourinho. Some distinguished football figures, including Arsène Wenger, thought he had got it wrong about Hunt's culpability too. It was not his finest hour. Later in the match, Carlo Cudicini, who had replaced Čech, was himself taken off with concussion after being challenged in the air by Ibrahima Sonko. Mourinho's ire was understandable in the heat of that moment. The surprise was that he nursed his wrath and carried it into the build-up to the first of two group matches with Barcelona.

Chelsea won that, through a Drogba goal, and drew 2–2 at Camp Nou thanks to the centre-forward's late response to Gudjohnsen putting Barcelona ahead. The first knockout round brought a sentimental journey to Porto, where Shevchenko struck (he was most effective in the cups) to earn a draw. Between this and the second leg, which Chelsea won 2–1, came that turbulent Carling Cup final in Cardiff. A late brawl saw John Obi Mikel sent off by Howard Webb along with Arsenal's Kolo Touré and Emmanuel Adebayor. Each club was fined £100,000 for failing to control its players.

Word had already begun to leak out that Abramovich and associates were becoming concerned about Chelsea's image. Speculation about a rift with Mourinho grew and eventually Mourinho began discussing it openly with friends and colleagues. But Chelsea had taken one of the four trophies available to them and were still in contention for the other three: a splendid distraction. It was against this background that Peter Kenyon, the chief executive, sought to assure the support that Mourinho would not leave. He said: 'José has a contract to 2010 and he wants to stay. We are not going to sack him. We support him, and given the level of speculation, where we are now is an even bigger achievement. Whatever you have read or heard, no list of candidates [to replace Mourinho] has been drawn up, no one has been offered the job. So let's put that one to bed. Hopefully, the speculation will stop and I think it should. As far as we are all concerned, the most important thing is that it is business as usual at Chelsea and we are putting all our energy into winning the three remaining trophies.'

By early April they had closed the gap at the top of the Premier League to three points by beating Tottenham while United went down to a Rio Ferdinand own goal at Portsmouth. They overcame Valencia to reach the Champions League semi-finals – and drew Liverpool again. Joe Cole's goal won the first leg at Stamford Bridge. Daniel Agger equalised on aggregate and the tie went to penalties. Anfield roared as Boudewijn Zenden, Xabi Alonso and Steven Gerrard scored. When Dirk Kuyt also netted he detonated an explosion because that was Liverpool through to the final; their goalkeeper, Pepe Reina, had saved from Arjen Robben and Geremi.

A few days later, all hope of retaining the domestic title evaporated as Mourinho's ten men could only draw 1–1 at Arsenal (Boulahrouz had been sent off). But there was still Wembley to come: the rebuilt Wembley, with its magnificent arch. A place that soared and sparkled

and seemed to have everything except a decent play-
ing surface. Not that Chelsea minded the lifeless pitch.
It seemed to suit them a lot more than United, whose
close-passing game kept breaking down, and aptly a long
ball led to Drogba settling matters in the 116th minute.
Drogba came second in the voting for Footballer of the
Year. Ronaldo won. United were top dogs again. And
Mourinho, who had looked just the man to see off Sir
Alex Ferguson, was himself about to bid farewell to
English football.

He ended the season with mixed feelings. There was
satisfaction in completing the clean sweep of English
trophies, as he later told one of his favourite British journalists, Duncan Castles, in an interview for the *Observer*.
'The FA Cup was so special,' he said. 'As as kid I grew up
watching FA Cup finals at Wembley and I was becoming frustrated at not having the FA Cup yet. So to win
it finally, especially after the very difficult season it had
been, was very special.' But he could still sense that the
end of his time at Stamford Bridge was nigh. Indeed he
considered leaving immediately after the Cup triumph
over Manchester United at Wembley and later declared
his decision to stay a while 'my biggest mistake'.

Summer of discontent

Things were not getting any easier for Mourinho, on or off the field. As if Arnesen, from whom he remained distant, were not enough, into the club that summer strode Avram Grant, the former manager of the Israeli national team and a friend of Abramovich who had been director of football at Portsmouth. He took the same job title at Chelsea. What Arnesen was called by then is hard to trace. He had begun as head of youth recruitment, nominally, but the 'youth' bit was soon dropped and he ended up as 'sporting director'. The reality was that Mourinho, from Grant's arrival in July 2007, was obliged to contend with not one but two directors of football. Even more unsettling for Mourinho – and the club's supporters – was a feeling that Grant, who had known Abramovich personally for some years and watched the Cup final with the owner in his box at Wembley, would be conveniently in place to take over the team; it was to prove well founded.

Mourinho's coterie had the impression that Grant would be working mainly with Shevchenko at first, helping the Ukrainian to recover his best form, but they could see the bigger writing on the wall; they knew that Abramovich yearned to have a more compliant creature in charge of the team and Grant fitted the description. On top of that, there was the respect factor. Mourinho was too highly regarded a coach to have Grant, whose credentials were relatively skimpy, foisted upon him, let alone groomed as his successor.

At first there was no sign of turbulence between them. As Grant took up his new post, the Chelsea squad flew to California to take part in a tournament featuring LA Galaxy, the Major League Soccer club for which David Beckham played, and Suwon Bluewings of South Korea. Abramovich was around the squad and, as he laughed and joked with Mourinho, a casual observer might have formed the view that here was an ideal owner/coach partnership. Yet it was soon to be broken, with another leading personality at the club taking a key role in the final scenes: John Terry, of all people. Mourinho had even lost the complete confidence of the captain who, in the best of times, had been his embodiment on the field but was now about to voice his disquiet. Terry, though his public image has taken a few dents over the years – not least when he was accused of having an affair with the former partner of Wayne Bridge, late of Chelsea and an England colleague, and stripped of the England captaincy by Fabio Capello – can be a deft manipulator of his fellow man, and a determined fighter of his corner, as was shown when Capello gave him the armband back after a year. Now he could be added to the ranks of the José-sceptics.

There was also the question of style, which Peter Kenyon confirmed was essential to Abramovich's quest – an anonymous associate of the owner was even quoted as saying they wanted to win 4–0 with the final goal being a volley from the edge of the penalty area! – and which Mourinho considered merely desirable. In any case, the coach said, in an apparent sideswipe at the quality of the squad with which he had been provided: 'It's all about omelettes and eggs. No eggs, no omelette. And it depends on the quality of the eggs. In the supermarket you have eggs class one, class two, class three. Some are more expensive than others and some give you better omelettes. So when the class-one eggs are in Waitrose and you cannot go there you have a problem.'

Nor, of course, can you make an omelette without breaking eggs, and Mourinho's relish for that part of the task was always an irritant to Abramovich according to Jason Burt of the *Daily Telegraph*, a leading member, like Duncan Castles, of a group of journalists, part of whose job is to penetrate the labyrinth that serves as Chelsea's corridors of power. 'For the first couple of years they got on quite well,' said Burt, 'but Abramovich got sick of Mourinho's aggressive behaviour. José's a typical

Portuguese male – he does like an argument. As soon as he went to Real Madrid, he began arguing with Jorge Valdano [the Spanish club's sporting director]. It's just the way he is. When Chelsea were winning, it didn't matter too much.' And then there was the Champions League: Abramovich's unfulfilled dream. Another season beckoned. A season in which it was so nearly to come true, and in the Russian's capital city, with Terry centrally involved in the final drama. But no Mourinho.

Thumbs down from Terry

The 2007–08 season started pleasantly enough with a 3–2 win over Birmingham City that broke a record, previously held by Bob Paisley's Liverpool, for consecutive home matches without defeat. Liverpool had put together a run of sixty-three between February 1978 and December 1980. This was Chelsea's sixty-fourth defence of their fortress. All but six of those matches had been under Mourinho. And he has always liked a favourable statistic. Chelsea then beat Reading away and drew at Liverpool. They beat Portsmouth but then lost at Aston Villa and could only draw goallessly at home to Blackburn Rovers, making their record just one win in four matches since Terry returned to the side after injury. The club had almost invariably lain first or second in the League from the day Mourinho took charge, but they were fifth in September when Rosenborg, from the Norwegian city of Trondheim, arrived at the Bridge for Chelsea's opening group match in the Champions League. This was when the Terry problem surfaced.

The background was that Mourinho had noticed a fall in Terry's physical performance and asked the club doctor, Bryan English, if there was any medical reason. English had then mentioned the inquiry to Terry, who had reacted angrily and refused to warm up for the Rosenborg match. When Terry and the rest of the team trailed into the dressing room at half-time a goal down, Mourinho snubbed the captain. It was not an ideal atmosphere, but Shevchenko equalised to produce a result that, while it could have been worse, was hardly the stuff of which European champions are made. Afterwards, Peter Kenyon went to Terry and asked his opinion of Mourinho's work. Terry's answer obliged the chief executive to relay it to Abramovich. Mourinho had been fatally undermined.

Two days later, on Thursday, 20 September, it was announced that he was leaving. By mutual consent, officially. We clamoured to know what was behind that intrinsically suspicious phrase and on the Sunday it came from the horse's mouth, via Duncan Castles, to whom Mourinho said: 'The Chelsea statement is correct. The relationship broke down, it is true, and "mutual agreement" is true. You know me. If I was sacked, I would say I was sacked. If I had closed the door, I would say I had closed the door. The relationship broke down not because of one detail or because of something that happened at a

certain moment. It broke down over a period of time.' So
he didn't feel undermined by Grant's arrival, even though
some in his camp had been reported to have regarded the
Israeli as a 'Mossad spy' on Abramovich's behalf? This
was after Grant had begun calling aside individual players
to ask them questions such as 'You look sad, why?', 'How
do you feel in this position?', 'Is this the best place for
you to play?' or 'Are we using your abilities well?' Some
might have called this being a director of football – albeit
one appearing to intrude on Mourinho's domain – and
others might indeed have regarded it as a form of internal
espionage. Surely, Castles asked, this had been like a stab
in the back? 'It doesn't matter to me,' Mourinho replied.
'I don't care. I don't care if I was stabbed in the back.
I really don't want to spend my time and energy fret-
ting about it.' And what about the trouble with Terry?
It had been no secret from the other players according
to Claude Makelele's autobiography, *Tout Simplement*, in
which the midfielder wrote: 'I met Rui [Faria], our physical trainer, and asked him if everything was OK. "No,
no, Claude. The rumours are true. The coach has been
fired." I asked him why and he explained a lot of players had complained about him, notably John Terry.' But
Mourinho had no criticism to make of John Terry either.
Nor is there any record of his having said a public word
since against Terry, who remains close to Abramovich
and has expressed a wish eventually to hold the post
once occupied for forty months by José Mourinho.

First Tottenham, then England

Mourinho exuded no false modesty about the void he would leave at Stamford Bridge, saying he would not return to say goodbye to the fans: 'Just imagine if I did – I would die in the crush out in the middle of the pitch.' As for his own feelings: 'I must admit I caught a tear. Just as a tear was coming out, I was catching it. I didn't want to cry, even though I felt like it. This was the most hurtful, painful experience of my career. My worst moment at any club anywhere.' He would be suppressing those tears all the way to the bank the next day. But first he went home to read and hear how much English football would miss him. 'How can I blame myself,' he rhetorically asked Duncan Castles, 'when the people are not happy that I'm going? The club is not happy [a questionable assertion]. The fans are not happy. My opponents are not happy. Even the referees are not happy – yes, a few of the referees have rung to say they are sad to see me go.'

One of these was Mark Halsey, who first encountered Mourinho when doing fourth-official duty for UEFA at a Champions League group match between Porto and Olympique Marseille in 2003. During Mourinho's time in England, they became friends and in 2008, when Halsey's wife, Michelle, was diagnosed with leukaemia, Mourinho arranged for the family to take a holiday in Portugal at his expense. The following August, when Mourinho was beginning his second season with Inter, it was announced that Halsey was suffering from lymphoma and had undergone surgery to remove a cancerous tumour from his throat. Before and after his recovery and return to Premier League refereeing, Mourinho kept in touch, inviting the family to Inter and then Real Madrid matches.

The day after leaving Chelsea, Mourinho was offered Martin Jol's job at Tottenham Hotspur. Jol was still in it. But everyone knew his days were numbered because Spurs officials had been photographed dining with the Sevilla coach Juande Ramos in Spain. Spurs had spent about £40 million on players, largely recommended by Damien Comolli, their director of football, during the summer and were in an ambitious frame of mind when they approached Mourinho offering to match his final Chelsea salary of £5.2 million a year. As they persisted in their entreaties, Mourinho kept negotiating with Chelsea, more than doubling the proposed payoff to himself and his coterie to £18 million, the bulk of which would naturally go into the Special One's account. In return he promised not to join another Premier League club for twelve months. Tottenham had served their purpose. Five weeks later they sacked Jol and brought in Ramos, who never settled in England despite a Carling Cup final triumph over Chelsea, by now managed by Avram Grant, and was in his turn replaced by Harry Redknapp.

Mourinho did have an opportunity to stay in England without breaking his agreement with Chelsea, for in early December the FA, looking for a successor to Steve McClaren as England manager after the failure to qualify for the European Championship of 2008, approached him. He said he was tempted until he realised the job would entail periods of inactivity and decided to wait for the right one, which happened to be in Italy. The FA proceeded to put an Italian, Fabio Capello, in charge of the England team.

While Mourinho was waiting for the call to San Siro, the club from whom he had parted did not exactly collapse. There was some excitable noise at first, much of it emanating from the predictable source of Didier Drogba, who told *France Football* magazine: 'I want to leave Chelsea. Nothing can stop me leaving now. Something is broken with the club. We all have the feeling that the story we have shared has finished too soon. We also have a feeling of helplessness. Everything hung on what the president [Abramovich] wanted. We are only employees. I made the mistake of putting too much feeling into the relationship with the manager.'

When you take this emotional outburst in the context of how Inter were to sink after Mourinho's departure for Real Madrid in 2010, you begin to gauge the power of the loyalty Mourinho can inspire. But Chelsea were not capsized like Inter by the great waves his departure caused. There was Terry to steady the ship. And Frank Lampard. And Drogba, who swallowed his disappointment as only two League matches were lost – against Manchester United at Old Trafford in Grant's first in charge, and later Arsenal at the Emirates Stadium – between late September and the end of the season. Furthermore, Chelsea got further than Mourinho had ever taken them in the Champions League – to the final, where, even after a petulant Drogba had been sent off, they would have beaten Manchester United on penalties but for Terry slipping on the artificial turf as he took his kick. They were also runners-up to United in the League.

But neither feat saved Grant from dismissal. Peter Kenyon, who, though his relationship with Mourinho had involved its share of storms, may have deemed his departure from the club premature (Mourinho always seemed to have more respect for Kenyon's footballing credentials than those of other Chelsea executives), left in the autumn of 2009 to pursue other ventures. Frank Arnesen lasted until November 2010, when it was announced that he had resigned but would not leave until the end of the season; in fact he left a couple of months early to start work as director of football at Hamburg. By then Chelsea were on their fourth manager since Mourinho, though there was almost daily, and well founded, speculation that Carlo Ancelotti might go the way of Grant and Luiz Felipe Scolari. Guus Hiddink had left of his own accord to return to international football. Manchester United still had the same manager. Sir Alex Ferguson had seen them all off and, after a run of consecutive English titles had been halted at three by Ancelotti's Chelsea, stormed back to win another in 2011.

Meanwhile Mourinho had resumed the friendly relations he had originally enjoyed with Abramovich. They had never done much socialising together in London because neither was a great socialiser, as Bruce Buck, the Chelsea chairman, once pointed out. Buck likes to joke that he and Abramovich are the joint owners of Chelsea: 'Roman has one million shares and I have one.' But the quietly spoken American lawyer is the most communicative member of the club's hierarchy. He said of Mourinho: 'If José's not working, he wants to be with his family.' And of Abramovich: 'Roman isn't very big on going to black-tie dinners and things. He tends to hang around with people he's known since his twenties, and they tend to be his Russian friends.' But they did begin to keep in touch after Mourinho left Chelsea. Six months into his fallow period, Mourinho accepted a gift of a limited-edition Ferrari worth £2 million from Abramovich and there have been occasional meetings since. There was even an offer to have his old job back which Mourinho politely declined in favour of his new obsession with restoring Real Madrid's supremacy over Barcelona. Pep Guardiola had earlier been contacted in case he fancied building a new Barcelona at the Bridge but he, too, preferred to stay in Spain. It is extraordinary to reflect that this was in the early spring of a year in which Chelsea, though they were knocked out of the Champions League by Mourinho's Inter, won the Double under Ancelotti.

Mark: my words

Before Mourinho and Guardiola clashed in the explosive Champions League semi-final of 2011, the customary invitation went out to Mark Halsey. By now the referee was back on the Premier League list and performing well. Had he gone to the first leg in Madrid, he might have felt sorry for Wolfgang Stark, the German official who had to keep control of a stormy affair in which one of Mourinho's players, Pepe, was sent off and the Barcelona reserve goalkeeper, Pinto, also red-carded after a scuffle at the mouth of the tunnel as the teams went off at half-time. But Halsey couldn't go to that one. He had promised his wife a short holiday in Devon – it was a glorious English spring – where he would be doing a run for charity and officiating at the League One match between Exeter City and Plymouth Argyle.

Halsey had been a semi-professional player. As a referee he reached Premier League level in 1999. Four years later, he travelled with Graham Poll and two linesmen to Porto for that Champions League fixture in which he first saw Didier Drogba – 'he was playing up front for Marseille and I remember thinking what a good player he was even then, very strong and quick' – and got to know Mourinho's ways. 'I'd never met this young man Mourinho before,' said Halsey, 'I'd seen a television programme about how he'd been assistant to Bobby Robson and then Louis van Gaal at Barcelona and thinking, "Wow, just learning the ropes from those kind of people," especially when he'd had no experience as a professional footballer whatsoever. Anyway, we just seemed to hit it off together. I was the fourth official and you know what José's like with his antics. He was just the same at Porto as he is now. But I used common sense, I handled him, and ever since he came to England we've been friends.'

Porto's first home match in the competition that season – that historic season in which they followed up success in the UEFA Cup the previous season by taking the big one – had been a 3–1 defeat, albeit at the distinguished hands of a Real Madrid team featuring the *galácticos* Roberto Carlos, Luis Figo, Ronaldo and Zinedine Zidane, but they had won 3–2 in Marseille and another victory over the French club, secured by a lone goal from Dmitri Aleinitchev, set them back on track for qualification for the knockout stages, in which they were to overcome Manchester United, Lyon, Deportivo La Coruña and, finally, Monaco.

After Mourinho had joined Chelsea, Halsey naturally refereed some of Chelsea's matches. 'He'd always shake my hand at the end and usually say, "Well done," although sometimes it'd be more a case of him coming on to the pitch and saying, "Hey, what about that penalty you missed for me?" and I do remember at Fulham once he came in at half-time and had a few words about a handball. He still thinks I should have given him a penalty in a match against Newcastle. So we've had our disagreements. But he's never spoken in an angry tone. I know, when he comes out on TV, people may think of him as a bit arrogant, but that's a long way from the truth as far as I'm concerned. He's never given the impression of being angry with me. I don't know why. I think he just likes my style of refereeing. He says he thinks of me as a twenty-third player on the pitch.'

In the last League match of Mourinho's third season with Chelsea, the title having been relinquished, Everton were the visitors to Stamford Bridge. Halsey was the referee. He arrived early and was spotted by Mourinho, who invited him into his office for coffee. Halsey recalled: 'He just said, "Come in, come in" and we sat down and spoke about football and refereeing decisions for about twenty or twenty-five minutes.' At the interval, Everton led through a goal from James Vaughan, but twelve minutes into the second half Didier Drogba equalised. David Moyes, the Everton manager, was furious, believing that Mikel Arteta had been fouled in the build-up. He marched on to the pitch to protest to Halsey and was redirected to the stands to watch the match finish in a draw.

Then came the Cup final and the summer, at the end of which Halsey renewed acquaintance with Mourinho in the Community Shield match, again between Chelsea and United, at Wembley. He showed yellow cards to three Chelsea players – Tal Ben Haim, Ricardo Carvalho and John Obi Mikel – along with Wayne Rooney during a 1–1 draw. United, for what it was worth, won on penalties. 'After the game he came up to me,' said Halsey. 'He just hugged me and said, "You are the top ref".'

A few weeks later, Mourinho was gone from English football. Halsey, apart from the seven months he spent out of the game due to illness, continued to referee Chelsea matches. 'I know the players who are still there hold him in the utmost respect,' he said. 'Sometimes, when I referee a Chelsea match, I speak to Didier Drogba and ask him about José: "Are you gonna join our friend next year?" He always just looks at me and smiles.'

In 2008, the Halsey family were struck the first of two blows when Michelle was found to have myeloid leukaemia. When Mourinho heard, he arranged for the family to stay at the five-star Lake Resort at Vilamoura on the Algarve. 'This was just fantastic,' said Halsey. 'This was a place that cost 600 euros a night! Obviously, if he'd still been at Chelsea, I wouldn't have gone. But for him just to go and do something like that – what can you say? He's been an absolute inspiration to me and my family, with his words and everything.' The following February, by which time Mourinho was more than half-way through his first season with Inter, Halsey visited Manchester with Michelle and their daughter, Lucy, for the second leg of a Champions League tie with United and joined the squad at their hotel before lunch. In the August came Halsey's own crisis. 'José kept in touch with me all the way through my treatment,' he said. 'I don't know how he found out about the illness, but he was very quickly on the phone. Wherever he's been, he's had my number and been in touch by phone, text or email. I remember when I was going through my treatment I sent him a picture message. Obviously I had no hair at the time. "Here's my latest picture," I said, and he replied, "At least you're better looking than Ray Wilkins!"'

Halsey, determined to return to the game, kept in shape and, in March 2010, having completed his treatment and got over the serious infection that followed, passed a referee's fitness test. His first match was between the reserve teams of Leicester City and Scunthorpe United and at the start of April he was awarded a League Two fixture between Rotherham United and Port Vale. When the new season started, he was restored to the Premier League, taking charge of the newcomers Blackpool as they began the campaign with the first of many surprises, beating Wigan Athletic 4–0 on their own ground, after both sets of supporters had given Halsey a warm reception. While he had been working his way back through the lower levels, there had been time to share in the burgeoning success of Mourinho's Inter.

Carlo Ancelotti, who had jousted with Mourinho in his first Inter season, coming off second best in a spiky Milan rivalry with one win to Mourinho's three as the *nerazurri* maintained a title-winning habit discovered under Roberto Mancini, renewed painful acquaintance when with Chelsea in the Champions League. But he could amply console himself with the domestic double, Didier Drogba's FA Cup final goal completing it after the League had been won in style. A style that would satisfy Roman Abramovich? You might think so. A century of League goals had been chalked up with the fifth of eight without reply from Wigan in the concluding match at the Bridge. There had earlier been seven against Stoke City, Aston Villa and Sunderland. But that Champions League departure at the hands of the man Abramovich had paid off rankled with the Russian. And now the European summit meeting was to be held in Chelsea's absence once more.

On 17 May 2010, Halsey held a dinner in aid of the Christie, a Manchester hospital specialising in the treatment of cancer. Mourinho could not be there. He was preparing Inter for the Champions League final against Bayern Munich, now coached by Mourinho's old teacher from the Barcelona days, Louis van Gaal. But he did have a DVD made and sent. It was played to hundreds of guests and an utterly unprepared Halsey, who sat back as Mourinho appeared on a giant screen with his now-trademark stubble and wearing Inter training kit. Mourinho looked into the camera and smiled.

'Hi, Mark,' he said. 'I used to be called, in your country, the Special One but, to be fair, you are the special one. Why? Because you are the only ref in the world I can say is my friend. Because "friend", for me, is a strong word. I know many referees and have good relations with lots of them, I respect lots of them, but "friend", in the real sense of the word, you are the only one. Why? Maybe because we have had a chance to see each other outside football a couple of times. Also because in this moment, and for the last three years, we have been in different countries and this cleans everything – you are a Premier League referee and I am not a Premier League manager. But especially because you are an incredible person. A top person – very honest, very polite, very friendly. When you were refereeing Chelsea, I won with you, I lost with you, I drew with you. So I wasn't winning all the time – I don't forget that against Newcastle you didn't see a penalty for Chelsea! But I'd always say you were player number twenty-three on the pitch, not a referee. And that is because of your mentality, your communication skills, your psychology. You are really one of the players. That is why everyone in the game respects you and likes you. And, finally, I could say "Congratulations" to you because you won again. But I don't say

"Congratulations". Because from the moment I know you had this problem I told you, "No problem for you. Easy for you." I know it wasn't easy. I know you fought a lot. But still I don't say, "Congratulations." Because, for winners, it's not necessary. Now you are back in football and I hope you can ref one of my matches. Because you are what I call you every time: "Top ref." You are the top ref.'

And, with a thumbs-up to Halsey, who by now was in tears, Mourinho headed back to the task of preparing Inter for their date with Bayern in the Bernabéu five days later. Halsey was there. Mourinho had laid on tickets for all his family. He had offered to pay for flights, a hotel too. 'I wouldn't have that,' said Halsey. 'Anyway, we were on holiday in Spain at the time, so we just booked into a little place in Madrid for a couple of days. We went to the hotel where Inter were staying. We pulled up outside in a taxi and there were all these guards and police and security men. So Michelle said, "We're not going to get in there," and I said, "We will." I took little Lucy and, as we walked up the steps, they all parted and let us through. There was José up on the balcony with all the players. He ran down and embraced me. My hair had grown back. It was very emotional. He'd been an inspiration to me during the illness. It was also quite funny because, when we arrived, he called me "top ref" as usual and some of the players who speak English came up and said, "Oh, so you're not fictional then! You are real! José talks about you all the time." And then they all came and shook my hand. Players and staff. It was fantastic. I love him to death, I really do.'

And there was still the big match to come.

Champions of Europe

It was a very, very big season for Inter because, although they had become almost accustomed to winning the Italian title – Mourinho, benefiting as Mancini had done from the liberal funding of Massimo Moratti, Inter's oil-rich owner, won his second to make it five in a row for the club – the latter of their two European titles had come in 1965. And Milan had taken no fewer than six since then, the most recent under Ancelotti in 2007.

In the previous season, Inter had made little headway in Europe, scraping through their opening group with a mere eight points before being dispatched by Manchester United, who won 2–0 at Old Trafford after a scoreless match at San Siro. Now the group-stage draw threw them in with Barcelona, the champions, who had beaten United at the end of Pep Guardiola's first season in charge, the bright young man emerging triumphant over the veteran Sir Alex Ferguson. Straight away Barcelona came to San Siro. There followed an excruciating goalless match, a phoney war between the giants of the group. Barcelona and Inter were confidently expected to qualify ahead of Dynamo Kiev and Rubin Kazan, the new force from Russia. But Rubin shocked Barcelona by winning there and the champions were under pressure to take three points from Mourinho's side at the Camp Nou. They stood up to it well, goals from Gérard Pique and Pedro barely reflecting their superiority on the night, and went on to top the group with victory in Kiev. Inter came second – and drew Chelsea in the first knockout round.

As always, the English press were looking forward to an encounter with Mourinho – and he didn't disappoint them. In the build-up to the first leg at San Siro, he first claimed to have all but single-handedly rebuilt Chelsea after arriving to discover that they had 'bought the wrong players' – Lampard? Makelele? Čech? Robben? – and declared that having been offered the England job had made him the proudest man in the world. Had he taken it, Mourinho would have had to deal with his former captain's frailty; John Terry had just been relieved of the England armband by Fabio Capello.

But now it was Terry's vulnerability on the pitch that Mourinho noted. The central defender gave Diego Milito space in which to shoot Inter into an early lead. Salomon Kalou was threatening to equalise when Walter Samuel brought him down. There was no penalty, no red card

– and, of course, no reaction from Mourinho, whose weekend histrionics during a Serie A match against Sampdoria in which Samuel and Ivan Cordoba were sent off had brought him a three-match dugout ban. Kalou did later bring Chelsea level, only for Esteban Cambiasso to score a spectacular second for Inter. And so it was off to the Bridge, where a strange pessimism pervaded the pre-match atmosphere. From Fulham Broadway tube station to the stadium, the talk among the Chelsea support was only of how their friend would somehow find a way to beat their team. The fans were right. And Inter deserved to win. They mounted a relentless physical challenge. Any Chelsea player in possession was harried without mercy. Creativity was near-impossible and, when Wesley Sneijder sent Samuel Eto'o through to score twelve minutes from the end, the home cause was lost. There was still time for Drogba to get himself sent off. As much as at any time since Mourinho had left, Chelsea looked to be missing him. As his barbed observation before the second leg had put it, he and the club had gone their separate ways: 'I keep winning things, they keep winning something ... the FA Cup.'

Yet the exit from Europe was to prove their path back to the League title as well that season. As Ancelotti's Chelsea marched towards the double, Mourinho's Inter waged a campaign on both the home and overseas fronts. They beat CSKA Moscow home and away to set up a semi-final meeting with Barcelona that was all the more piquant for the deal the previous summer that had seen Mourinho's club swap Zlatan Ibrahimovic, the much-debated but undeniably prolific Swede, for Eto'o and £40 million. Eto'o emerged by far the more successful signing, though it was Sneijder, arguably the star of the European season, who cancelled out Pedro's opening goal at San Siro and Maicon, the attacking right-back, and Milito who gave Inter a 3–1 advantage.

The Camp Nou was less fearful of Mourinho than Stamford Bridge had been. But he still silenced it, even after Thiago Motta, the Brazilian midfield blocker, had been sent off in the first half for pushing a hand into the face of Sergio Busquets, who promptly collapsed and infamously peeked from between his hands to check that Motta had been red-carded by Frank de Bleeckere, the Belgian referee. Mourinho swept up a scornful arm. But he had come to 'park the bus' (to borrow the phrase he used at Chelsea once when Tottenham came in ultra-defensive mood) and such a tactic can work with ten men. Inter made it work, not even attempting to get to the other end of the field, and there were just seven minutes left when Gérard Pique scored the only goal of the match. Inter were through to the final and, after De Bleeckere's whistle had confirmed it, as the Barcelona anthem plaintively rang round the vast bowl, Mourinho ran on to the pitch and, fiercely staring, stood pointing in solidarity to the Italian fans on the top tier. It was too much for Victor Valdes, the goalkeeper attempting to restrain him before himself being escorted away. Mourinho then left the field and went to the little chapel in the bowels of Barcelona's stadium and wept. Back in the dressing room, most of his players were in tears. Once they had composed themselves, they emerged to pay tribute to the coach's rigorous preparation.

He, and they, would have to do it all over again if the trophy was to be lifted in Madrid, where they were to face Bayern Munich, coached by Mourinho's former Barcelona boss Louis van Gaal. They greeted each other with a cordial embrace before the kick-off. Bayern began brightly and Martin Demichelis, with a header from a corner, and Mourinho's old friend Arjen Robben might have put them in front. But Milito made them rue those misses when, played in by Sneijder, he coolly waited for the Bayern goalkeeper, Hans-Jorg Butt, to commit himself before lifting the ball into the net. Mourinho's keeper, Júlio César, then underlined his importance to the side by denying Thomas Müller as Robben continued to probe the Inter defence, so troubling Christian Chivu at left-back that Mourinho was obliged to switch his vastly experienced captain, Javier Zanetti, to the task. But Bayern left just enough space at the back for Inter to attack on the break and, with twenty minutes left, Eto'o slipped Milito through for his second goal of the night. It was the Argentine's sixth in eleven Champions League matches. Naturally he was central to the celebrations that followed.

While a testy Van Gaal complained that the more creative team had lost to mere counter-attackers, Mourinho basked in the glory of having won the European title with two clubs. He had done it previously with Porto and Van Gaal with Ajax (whose youngsters had been victorious over Milan in 1995). So the pupil had beaten his teacher to a distinction previously achieved only by Ernst Happel (Feyenoord 1970 and Hamburg 1983) and Ottmar Hitzfeld (Borussia Dortmund 1997 and Bayern 2001). He was well aware of all the historical implications of Inter's win: of how, when they last took the title by beating Benfica on the home soil of San Siro in 1965 (Real Madrid had been overcome in Vienna a year earlier), the club's patron had been Moratti's father, Angelo; and certainly of what lay before him, including the possibility of guiding a third club to Europe's pinnacle before he reached the age of fifty at the end of January 2013. That gave him two seasons and such was the Mourinhomania that lingered after the crowds had drifted away from the Bernabéu that it seemed almost odds-on.

For Mourinho was to stay at the Bernabéu. It was an open secret that, just as he had left Porto after winning the Champions League, he was to walk away from Inter – with equal honour, it transpired – to join Europe's most garlanded club of all. Within days, Florentino Peréz, the president of Real Madrid, had duly tendered a contract for him to sign and a new chapter had begun.

The *nerazzurri* hordes would never forget his two

years with them. True, he could be said to have fixed something that was hardly broken, for Inter had become accustomed to Serie A titles before Roberto Mancini's surprising resignation. But to transform them into a European force, to elevate them to a perch that had become unfamiliar to Italian clubs with the all-too-obvious exception of the *rossoneri* of Milan, was quite something. Something they were to lose almost as soon as he left.

The rebuilding job

When, in the summer of 2008, he installed his family in a house near the Swiss border and began work at Inter's lovely training ground near the small town of Appiano Gentile, there was hardly an Italian to be seen around the place. Not on the playing staff anyway: only one Italian, Marco Materazzi, the ageing warrior once of Everton but probably best known for having so incensed Zinedine Zidane in the 2006 World Cup final that the great Frenchman butted him in the chest and was sent off, was among the fourteen who appeared in Mourinho's first Champions League match with the club, a 2–0 victory over Panathinaikos in Athens. Latin Americans were in the majority with five Brazilians including Júlio César and Maicon, Zanetti and Cambiasso from Argentina and Ivan Cordoba from Colombia and that was not radically to change, for Materazzi was also the sole Italian to appear in the triumph in Madrid some twenty months later, coming on for Milito in a sentimental substitution a couple of minutes from the final whistle. The fourteen that night featured four Argentines, including Milito, and three Brazilians. But maybe the catalyst for change, the key to the transformation – Mourinho aside, of course – had been the second of two Africans to arrive in successive summers.

Sulley Muntari, the Ghanaian midfield player, had been signed almost as soon as Mourinho joined the club, along with Ricardo Quaresma, a Portugal winger apparently destined to disappoint, and Mancini, a very quick Brazilian who also played wide and failed to last at the club. But the truly significant signings were made a year later when the sale of Ibrahimovic for an estimated £60 million, including the value put on Eto'o, did much to fund the arrival of not only the Cameroonian striker but Sneijder, a snip at £13 million from Real Madrid, Milito, the outstanding Brazilian defender Lucio, and Goran Pandev, the clever Macedonian, all of whom conspired in the eventual triumph over Bayern. For Mourinho to have integrated them into the most effective unit in European football in just a year was extraordinary.

But he didn't plan it that way. Nor could he be credited with genius in the transfer market as well as on the training field. Because, having initially built his team around Ibrahimovic, he would have been happy to continue with such a policy at the front. Until it became clear that Ibrahimovic had his heart set on that move to Barcelona. Pep Guardiola was equally keen to offload Eto'o, with whom he had fallen out. So that was the start of it. As for Milito and Thiago Motta, their moves from Sampdoria had already been arranged by Marco Branca, who, as Inter's sporting director, supervised recruitment. Lucio might not have been signed from Bayern Munich if Mourinho had been granted his wish to bring Ricardo Carvalho from Chelsea (he had even tried to relieve his former club of Frank Lampard the previous summer, before settling for Muntari).

Where Mourinho did come up with a masterstroke was in realising that Ibrahimovic, who, with his majestic technique, could both create and finish, had to be replaced by two men. Hence the move for Sneijder, whom he resolved to put in the space behind Milito in the now fashionable 4–2–3–1 formation. He had devised the right method of play. And the rest, the drilling, was Mourinho's meat and drink. The team was, as ever with Mourinho, built on a defence of military precision, protected by the likes of Cambiasso and, when available, Thiago Motta, as if their lives depended on it. Sneijder operated in what, recalling Porto, you might call the Deco role. He was principally responsible for unlocking the defences of opponents, Milito and Eto'o for finishing. Eto'o was impressively disciplined on the right. He was not the first big-name player to understand that doing things Mourinho's way led to winners' medals. In Madrid he won his third in the Champions League, after 2006 and 2009 with Barcelona.

As Inter developed in Mourinho's second season, the Italians were treated to a familiar manifestation of his style. In the December, after a less than impressive draw with Atalanta in which Sneijder had been sent off, Mourinho was sitting on the team bus when he spotted a newspaper journalist in the space next to the bus reserved for interviews with the club's in-house television station. Mourinho leapt off the bus and had sharp words with the journalist, who, it turned out, had been there legitimately. By the time Mourinho had apologised, everyone had forgotten the team's performance and the dismissal of the coach's key signing. Milito may have been alluding to such episodes when he said of Mourinho: 'There is no coach like him when it comes to ... reducing the tension within the team when things aren't going well.'

Vieira: the value of trust

Patrick Vieira had known what to expect. He had done battle for Arsenal against Mourinho's Chelsea and been told by Claude Makelele that he would enjoy working with him. 'Claude was right,' said Vieira. 'He was a winner, first and foremost, but very clear and honest in his dealings with the players. We really took to him. When he arrived, I had a difficult time with injuries, but he established a trust between us. The trust between a manager and a player on the pitch is one thing. The trust off the pitch is another. And he assured me that I would be given time to get back to my best. He was fantastic with me. He made everything very clear. He made sure that no decision he made ever came as a surprise to me. That is very important. When he came to the club, the team was playing for Ibrahimovic. Because he was the man – he was the player making the difference in games. And for the first year of Mourinho it stayed that way. But then Mourinho changed things and it became a team of collective rather than individual effort.'

The visit to Old Trafford in March 2009, when Nemanja Vidic scored early and Cristiano Ronaldo made it 2–0 shortly after Vieira's replacement by Sulley Muntari, was a significant milestone. 'I think it told Mourinho what was needed,' said Vieira. 'It showed him which aspects of the team he needed to improve if we were to have a chance of winning the Champions League. And he did that at the end of the season.'

The next Champions League campaign featured Vieira as, at best, a substitute in the group stages and in the January he left, at the age of thirty-three, to rejoin Roberto Mancini at Manchester City, where the Italian had succeeded Mark Hughes. In Manchester, he was also to renew acquaintance with a twenty-year-old Mario Balotelli, who moved from Inter at the end of the season, after the Champions League triumph. Vieira's memories of Inter remain fond, and much of that is to do with Mourinho. 'Of course he had two or three players he could count on specially,' said Vieira. 'Zanetti, for instance. That was very important. But he made everyone feel they were trusted and that he believed in them. He was very close to his players. Between training sessions, you would be at lunch and he would take his plate and come and join you at the table. It's important when you can create such an atmosphere between a manager and his players – really close, really trusting. I think that is why players perform for him. They are dedicated to him.'

There was also a bond between Mourinho and Moratti that may have helped Inter to achieve their objectives. 'You have two big personalities there,' said Vieira. And none of the tension that existed between Mourinho and Abramovich? If it existed, Vieira never saw it. 'And, because of what they won together, there will always be a special relationship with Moratti, just as with the players. As for Moratti's relationship with the players, it is like that of a father with his sons. He really loves the players and is close to them. And I don't know a single player who has left Inter and not been sad because they are leaving Moratti.'

Several months before Vieira left, a departure from the off-the-field team had been André Villas-Boas. He had remained a member of Mourinho's staff along with Silvino Louro and Rui Faria but yearned to strike out in his own right and, to this end, went home to Portugal in the summer of 2009. He was thity-one now and within a couple of months had found his job at Academica. The next summer 'Mini-Mourinho' – how Villas-Boas hated that nickname – was invited to Porto and his team were still unbeaten in both domestic and European competition when they clinched the Portuguese league with several matches to spare. When they overcame Braga, also from northern Portugal, in the Europa League final in Dublin, the echoes of Mourinho could hardly have been more resonant. Yet Villas-Boas always took care to maintain a distance and, to give him his due, his Porto had a much more attacking style than Mourinho's. Already Villas-Boas was being tipped for leading jobs in England. He was, of course, on the radar of Roman Abramovich and, when the call came to return to Stamford Bridge in Mourinho's erstwhile role, all of his commendable intentions to give Porto at least one more season went out the window.

England, his England

A recurrent Italian reservation about Mourinho was that his heart wasn't really in the country's football because so much of it remained in England and in November 2009, a week after Inter had boosted their chances of qualifying for the knockout stages of the Champions League with a gritty win in Kiev, he told me in an interview – at least I thought it was an interview – that he hoped to spend the next phase of his career back in the Premier League.

It was during an international break, when most of his players were away from Appiano Gentile. The workload was light and he had agreed to see me in connection with a biography of Sir Alex Ferguson, to whom he was only too eager to pay tribute. He mentioned having first met Ferguson when a humble interpreter for Sir Bobby Robson at Barcelona in 1996. Ferguson had come with Manchester United's chairman, Martin Edwards, and a senior director, Maurice Watkins, to buy Jordi Cruyff, and as the big hitters from both of these huge clubs sat round a table in a restaurant arranging the deal, Mourinho noticed how centrally involved Ferguson was in the talks. 'He was fighting hard for his club,' Mourinho recalled, 'and an understanding of that dimension of management made me take an even greater interest in the English game, to fall in love with it even before I came.' Later in our talk, he explained why England still attracted him. 'I want to work with a different perspective,' he said. 'At Porto, my objective was to earn the right to go abroad. At Chelsea, my ambition was to create a little bit of history [the club had not been champions of England for half a century]. But I always knew Chelsea lacked the normal English culture of stability. I was never under any illusions. I understood the personality of Roman and the people around him [he carefully exempted Peter Kenyon from this] and knew that it was not a job for ten years. My role was to give this man what he wanted – victory – knowing that, sooner or later, my time would finish, because there were too many things going on around me. In Italy, I was coming to the motherland of tactics, the country of *catennacio* [literally door-bolt] and defensive football. The objective was to win not only in a third different league but a place where they say foreign coaches have little success. But the time will come for stability.'

Stability? What he meant was that England's leading clubs had long-term managers: Ferguson had been at United since 1986, Arsène Wenger at Arsenal since

1996, and even Rafael Benítez had been at often-troubled Liverpool for more than five years, since the same summer of 2004 in which Mourinho had arrived at Chelsea. While clearly it was unrealistic to hope to match Ferguson's one-club longevity, he did have a wish to build as he and Wenger had done. Mourinho added: 'I love Inter and would love to build for the future here. In fact, I am doing it now because I am not a selfish coach and I'm thinking about the future in terms of youth development and the age structure of my team – but Italy is not the country for this. England is the country. And my football is English football.'

Why had he begun to talk about his own career? I came to the conclusion that he would not mind my informing the readers of *The Times*. After all, such material, even if it were intended to address the inspiration of Ferguson, would hardly have kept for a biography not due to be published until the autumn of 2010 (by which time he had indeed left Inter, albeit not for England but for Spain and the challenge of a fourth league). *The Times* used my piece on its front page and, naturally, it caused even more of a stir in Italy than England. Within hours, Mourinho had issued a statement to the effect that he had not spoken to any newspaper but to the author of a book. I could only confirm this. But he didn't seem too put out. The theme persisted and in the January he felt obliged to clear things up: 'Yes, I love English football and the idea of going back to live in England. I want to go back and will do one day – that's 100 per cent certain. But I have no idea when that will be. Anyway, I would never leave a job half-fulfilled.' He didn't require the full span of a contract lasting until 2012 – and by now worth an estimated £10 million a year – to finish the job. That European title was just four months away.

It was amusing to recall on the glorious night, as the Bernabéu turned an exultant blue and black, that when we had met back in November, during the international break, Mourinho had received a text message from Ferguson, whose United were strolling through their Champions League group, already qualified with two matches to spare and unaware of the threat Bayern would later pose. 'Do you fancy meeting in Madrid in May?' it concluded. Mourinho made the date. Ferguson didn't, though his time was to come in London a year later, when now Mourinho missed the bus that was instead taken by Pep Guardiola and Barcelona.

Wesley, you look tired

Outside the Bernabéu on the night Inter became champions of Europe, there had been a telling scene. The engine of the team bus was ticking over, throbbing as the team waited to be taken for their celebratory meal. They had a more important matter on their minds for, after Zanetti had presented Mourinho with his captain's armband, a plea to stay and 'continue our battles' was handed over on behalf of everyone. Mourinho, much moved, walked off the bus and was ushered into a car, which had taken him only a few yards when it stopped. He had spotted the lone figure of the tall Materazzi, his white top brilliant against the wall on which he leant next to the bus. Mourinho went to the veteran defender and, as they tenderly embraced, Mourinho confirmed that he would be leaving. 'What am I to do?' asked Materazzi. 'Retire? After you, I can't have another coach.' Mourinho gently eased away. He was in tears. 'Keep calm, José,' said a solicitous Frits Ahlstrom, the UEFA liaison officer, leading him off to another round of media work.

And yet Materazzi (who no more retired, of course, than Didier Drogba left Chelsea in the wake of Mourinho) had become just a squad player, as his cameo appearance in the final had emphasised. The whole squad were to miss Mourinho, and so badly that his successor, Rafael Benítez, whose time at Liverpool had expired at the end of the 2009–10 season, lasted only a few months. The Spaniard was sacked two days before Christmas and replaced by Leonardo, the former Milan coach. No longer did Sneijder, Milito and company carry all before them, though they had survived the Champions League group stage despite a sound defeat at Tottenham. In Serie A, they trailed a long way behind Milan.

Sneijder, along with Lucio and Maicon, were able to take a couple of January days off to attend the Ballon d'Or ceremony in Zurich, where they were named in FIFA's team of the year. Coach of the Year was Mourinho, who sat in the audience as Sneijder declared: 'For me it was an amazing year. It could have been better – because I wanted to win the World Cup – but first of all it was a pleasure to work with José Mourinho, and I want to tell him this on stage, that he is for me the best coach in the world.' Mourinho swallowed and once again his eyes were moist. An insight into the special relationship between Mourinho and players had earlier been given by Sneijder when he said: 'Once he told me "Wesley, you look tired, take some days off, go to the sun with your wife and daughter." All other coaches just talked about training, but he sent me to the beach. So I went to Ibiza for three days and, when I was back, I was ready to kill and die for him.' Even Zlatan Ibrahimovic, after he had left for Barcelona, said that: 'At Inter with José Mourinho, I could go out and kill for him – that was the motivation he gave me.'

Without it, Inter were just another Serie A team in the Champions League knockout stages: beatable. They were removed in the quarter-finals by Schalke, the mid-table German side running up a 7–3 aggregate score that was made to look even less flattering to Inter when Manchester United then strolled to a 2–0 victory over Schalke in Gelsenkirchen before Ferguson brought in his squad players for an equally comfortable 4–1 win at Old Trafford. Mourinho meanwhile, was doing his enemy-of-football routine as Real Madrid lost to Barcelona. Some observers thought he had thereby ruled himself out of the United job when Ferguson retired. Others, noting the Ferguson antics that had brought the Scot a five-match dugout suspension by the FA, might have believed him more appropriately qualified than ever.

Index

Index

Index